NONBOOK MATERIALS
The Organization of Integrated Collections

Second Edition

Jean Weihs
with Shirley Lewis and Janet Macdonald

in consultation with the
CLA/ALA/AECT/AMTEC Advisory Committee on the
Cataloguing of Nonbook Materials

62755

Canadian Library Association, 1979

Printed and bound in Canada

Canadian Cataloguing in Publication Data

Weihs, Jean, 1930-
 Nonbook materials

  Bibliography: p.
  ISBN 0-88802-130-5

1. Cataloging of non-book materials—Handbooks, manuals, etc.
I. Lewis, Shirley, 1935-   II. Macdonald, Janet, 1936-
III. Canadian Library Association.   IV. Joint Advisory Committee
on Nonbook Materials.

Z695.66.W44 1979   0.25.3'4   C79-090075-0

Joint Advisory Committee on Nonbook Materials

Chairpersons
Dr. Nancy Williamson, 1977–
Suzanne Massonneau, 1975–1977

American Library Association representatives
Peter Deekle,   1978–
Head, Nonprint Media Services,
University of Maryland Libraries.

Suzanne Massonneau,   1974–1978
Assistant Director for Technical Services,
Guy W. Bailey Library,
University of Vermont.

Vivian L. Schrader,
Head, Audiovisual Section,
Descriptive Cataloging Division,
Library of Congress.

**Association for Educational Communications
and Technology representatives**
Various members of AECT have attended and
contributed to Committee meetings.

**Association for Media and Technology in
Education in Canada representative**
Larry Moore,
Associate Professor, School Librarianship,
Faculty of Education,
Queen's University.

Canadian Library Association representatives
J. McRee Elrod,
Director,
Special Libraries Cataloguing, Inc.

Nancy Williamson,
Associate Professor,
Faculty of Library Science,
University of Toronto.

**The authors of Nonbook Materials: The
Organization of Integrated Collections**
Shirley Lewis,
Deputy Director,
Brampton Public Library.

Janet Macdonald,
Co-ordinator, Audiovisual Services,
North York Public Library.

Jean Weihs,
Course Director, Library Techniques,
Seneca College of Applied Arts and Technology.

Foreword

Increasing emphasis on cultural, educational, and recreational activities, together with the continuous impact of mass media on contemporary life, has led many segments of our society to the recognition of the vital importance of optimum access to information. As a result, it has become the responsibility of librarians and media specialists to ensure the best possible access, whether the need is related to a general request or a specific enquiry, and regardless of the physical format in which the information is presented. To this end, the general objective is the organization of all kinds of physical units of information for successful retrieval as quickly, efficiently, and economically as possible.

In meeting the general objective, the librarian or media specialist must be mindful of the fact that users are a heterogeneous group of people who, individually, may approach the same information in a variety of ways. One solution to the problem is to arrange the physical units in a systematic linear sequence. However, since information is of multi-dimensional nature, this alone will not satisfy all user requirements. Traditionally, the library catalogue has been designed to complement and supplement the physical arrangement of information units. In doing so, the catalogue has been designed to fulfill three fundamental objectives — the location of an item about which some specific detail is known; the gathering and relating of items which have informational characteristics in common; and the description of each item in sufficient detail to allow a user to identify it as the item he requires, or to make a choice among items containing similar information. To accomplish these objectives, library and resource centre catalogues must be constructed on a consistent and systematic basis. While, with respect to printed materials, cataloguing codes for this purpose have existed for many years, it is only since the middle of the twentieth century that nonbook materials have been recognized as performing an informational function of a magnitude considered to be equal to that of monographs and serials. Moreover, it is only with the publication of the second edition of *Anglo-American Cataloguing Rules* that libraries and resource centres have finally been provided with a truly comprehensive and integrated approach to the organization of all informational materials.

When the authors were preparing the preliminary and first editions of this manual, they were developing a pioneering effort in which it was their primary purpose to identify and examine all opinions and views in any way pertinent to the problems of nonbook materials and to select and present in a manual of practice solutions which they considered to be most viable. As such, these earlier editions provided a logical and systematic approach to the organization of nonbook materials which has received both national and international recognition. Testimony to this is the fact that in conjunction with *Non-book Materials Cataloguing Rules*, prepared by the Library Association Media Cataloguing Committee, and the 4th edition of *Standards for Cataloging Non-print Materials; An Interpretation and Practical Application*, by Alma Tillin and William J. Quinly, the 1st edition of *Nonbook Materials: the Organization of Integrated Collections* was one of the primary sources for the development of rules for nonbook materials in *AACR2*. Since principles and fundamental rules for the cataloguing of nonbook materials as presently understood have now been consolidated, the role of this second edition of *Nonbook Materials* differs from that of its predecessors. It continues to be a manual of practice, but as an interpretation and explication of principles and rules set out in *AACR2*. In this respect it is anticipated that it will serve as a companion volume to that Code.

In the preparation of all the editions of this manual, the authors have consulted and sought advice from many sources, local, national, and international, and have endeavoured to present a pragmatic approach to the organization problems of nonbook materials. The major support for this work came from the Joint Advisory Committee which was formed prior to the publication of the first edition to work with the authors in an advisory and consultative capacity. The Committee members, who were representative of several national organizations in Canada and the United States interested in the library and media fields, served as technical consultants and acted in a liaison capacity, keeping their organizations informed, transmitting their views to the authors, and exchanging ideas and viewpoints to ensure representation of the needs of numerous kinds of libraries and instructional media centres. In doing so, the Joint Advisory Committee concerned itself with setting practice into a sound theoretical framework — a framework which was compatible with *AACR1* and which solidified and contributed to the material results in *AACR2*.

While this work truly represents the work of the authors, it is also the result of a successful experiment in international cooperation, in which the Committee has been conscientious and dedicated to the task of making order out of chaos. Nevertheless, while a threshold of standardization has been achieved, the Committee recognizes that, by nature, the field of nonprint media remains very volatile and that computer technology will point to new modes of information handling in the future. Thus, it is almost a foregone conclusion that the last word on nonbook materials has not been spoken. The Committee views this second edition of *Nonbook Materials* as one more step on a continuum of progress in the recognition and use of nonprint media as a source of information. As deliberations on the problems of organizing nonprint media move into the future, the Committee hopes that this work will serve as a starting point for discussion and future development of principles and rules and that the channels of communications in international cooperation will be kept open.

Nancy J. Williamson,
Chairperson of the Joint Advisory Committee,
Associate Professor of Library Science,
Faculty of Library Science,
University of Toronto.

Acknowledgements

It is impossible to detail the many contributions made by individuals and organizations to this work. We are indebted to the Joint Advisory Committee on Nonbook Materials and its chairpersons, Dr. Nancy Williamson (1977-1979), Suzanne Massonneau (1975-1977), and Dr. Margaret Chisholm (1970-1975) for encouragement, information, and constructive criticism. The support provided by the American Library Association, the Association for Educational Communications and Technology, the Association for Media and Technology in Education of Canada, and the Canadian Library Association through their representatives on the Joint Advisory Committee has been invaluable. Their continuing interest in international standards for nonbook materials cataloguing was also an important impetus to the revision of the *Anglo-American Cataloguing Rules*, 2nd edition.

Many librarians, media specialists, and other professionals with expertise in specific fields have contributed information to this work. We have appreciated their help. A few contributed more than could be expected of friendship, professional concern, or duty. To these people we send our special thank you: Dr. Ronald Hagler who provided continuing help and who commented on the final manuscript; Edwin Buchinski who provided an opportunity to have opinions on nonbook cataloguing presented to appropriate committees; Lorraine Steele who typed willingly without remuneration; Ben Tucker, Liz Bishoff, and David Remington who attended many Joint Advisory Committee meetings and offered helpful comments; and Harry Weihs who edited the final manuscript.

The research assistant for the first edition, Frederick Weihs, had his name omitted inadvertently from that work. We wish to acknowledge his contribution to some of the basic research done for that edition.

As with the first edition, we were pleased by the number of letters we received from librarians and media specialists from many parts of the world. The questions asked and the suggestions made were valuable input for this work. Comments on this edition are welcomed and should be addressed to Jean Weihs, c/o Canadian Library Association, 151 Sparks St., Ottawa, Canada K1P 5E3.

Jean Weihs
Shirley Lewis
Janet Macdonald

Table of Contents

Introduction

Nonbook Materials: The Organization of Integrated Collections has been revised to keep it abreast of the latest cataloguing practices as described in the second edition of the *Anglo-American Cataloguing Rules*. However, this edition is based on the same principles that were stated in the introduction to the first edition.

It has been written for all types of libraries and media centres which wish to have an all-media catalogue, i.e., one in which the entries for all materials, both book and nonbook, are interfiled. The second edition of the *Anglo-American Cataloguing Rules* makes this task much easier to accomplish than did the first edition because it prescribes the same rules of entry and description for all materials.

This edition, like the first edition of *Nonbook Materials: the Organization of Integrated Collections*, can be used by libraries and media centres which prefer to file and/or store their collections by type of material. However, the authors advocate the integration of collections, both in the catalogue and on the shelves, because they believe that this results in the best public service. The catalogue should be as easy and convenient for the patron to use as possible, without sacrificing the effectiveness of information retrieval. Many patrons, through ignorance or lack of time, are unable to look through several files in different places. Indeed, many are unaware that they have a choice of media in their subject field. The public is best served when entries for all materials in the collection are interfiled in one catalogue. Inter-shelving of all materials is advocated in the section on storage. The authors' informal experiments, letters received, and journal articles (see page 116) point to the increased use of all materials, book as well as nonbook, when the collection is intershelved.

This book presupposes a knowledge of book cataloguing and basic cataloguing principles. No attempt has been made to duplicate the *Anglo-American Cataloguing Rules*, 2nd edition; rather, the rules pertaining to nonbook materials have been collected and, in some instances, expanded.

It is difficult to provide rules for all the formats now on the market or to predict media yet to be developed. If a cataloguer encounters a format not covered by the rules in this book, she/he should follow the general rules as closely as possible and find specific solutions in ways suggested on pages 123 to 126.

The catalogue card format has been used in examples throughout this book because it makes the examples easily recognizable and adds a subject analysis dimension to the cataloguing. Card catalogues and book catalogues are slowly giving way to computer output microform (COM) catalogues and on-line catalogues, but the same cataloguing principles are applied and, therefore, the samples are valid whatever form of catalogue a media centre uses.

The *Anglo-American Cataloguing Rules*, 2nd edition, allows three levels of description (see pages 11 to 13). The cataloguer must work within the framework of the individual media centre's policy with regard to the amount of information to be put in the catalogue record. The amount of information and the amount of research required to obtain this information, if it is not readily available, must be balanced against the value of the information to the patron. Inexpensive, limited information cataloguing can be just as costly in terms of public service staff time as detailed cataloguing in terms of technical service staff time.

Cataloguing Policy for Nonbook Materials

Cataloguing Policy for Media Centres

In order to establish cataloguing procedures for an integrated collection, a media centre must make policy decisions which will apply to all its materials. These will include:

- a classification scheme;
- the depth of classification within the scheme;
- a numbering system such as Cutter numbers or call letters;
- a subject heading system;
- the extent and detail of descriptive cataloguing and added entries.

Decisions also need to be made about the extent and type of involvement in external cataloguing. If a media centre wishes to use commercial and/or centralized cataloguing services, it is wise to select a service which adheres to standard practice for book and nonbook materials. These services are likely to provide a standard of cataloguing which will appeal to the largest market. Therefore, detailed cataloguing may be supplied since it is easier to delete or ignore items in the record which are not particularly useful than to add items which are needed.

Automated cataloguing networks are expanding. Participation in such a network will necessitate the use of standard cataloguing by each member.

New media centres and those planning policy changes should consider the following points in determining cataloguing procedures.

I. DESCRIPTION AND HEADINGS

Nationally and internationally recognized rules for descriptive cataloguing should be applied if a media centre plans to make full use of any external bibliographic aids, e.g., cataloguing tools. Therefore, the *Anglo-American Cataloguing Rules*, 2nd edition, should be used.

A. The Cataloguing of Materials as Individual Items or Sets

Many materials are sold in sets and can be processed either as units or as separate items with a series added entry indicating their relationship.

In deciding whether to keep a set together or to break it up and catalogue each item separately, the cataloguer must consider the type of materials, the media centre, and the needs of the user. Subject analysis often affects the decision. If each item within a set would have significantly different classification numbers and subject headings, it may be advantageous to catalogue each part of the set separately. Sample card 18 is an example of this. Other titles in the "A Closer look into history" series are "The Order of the Garter," "The Crusades," "A Look at English law," etc. The titles in this series may be more useful catalogued as separate items.

On the other hand, if each item within a set would have the same classification and subject headings, it is probably more efficient to catalogue the series as a unit. Sample card 17 is an example of this.

B. Added Entries

The purpose of added entries is to enable a catalogue user to find a particular item by some name or title other than the main entry heading. Added entries also group materials in useful ways, e.g., by director. The number and kind of added entries required depends on the nature of catalogue use in each media centre. The following points should be considered when establishing a policy for added entries:

1. An added entry policy should be applied consistently to book and nonbook materials.
2. The policy should be in keeping with the chosen level of description, e.g., more entries in 3rd level description than in 1st level.
3. Only names, titles, and series listed in the catalogue record are traced. Added entries may be made for any one or all of these if the cataloguer believes that a patron may search for an item under a particular heading(s).

II. SUBJECT ANALYSIS

The subject analysis systems chosen by a library for its book collection should be used for all media.

A. Subject Headings

Preference should be given to a subject heading system which is comprehensive and periodically revised. The systems used most commonly by certain types of media centres are mentioned below.

Library of Congress subject headings are used in many academic, research and special libraries. Special libraries devoted to specific disciplines may use subject-oriented, authoritative, updated lists, e.g., MeSH (Medical Subject Headings) headings for health science collections.

Library of Congress subject headings are also used in large adult collections in many public libraries and secondary school media centres. Most centres with small collections report the use of Sears subject headings. However, those with large growth potential tend to use Library of Congress headings even though their collections may remain small for a few years.

Juvenile collections in public libraries and elementary school media centres generally use Sears subject headings. However, some media centres have adopted Library of Congress *Subject Headings for Children's Literature*, which has been endorsed as the national standard by the Cataloging and Classification Section Executive Committee of the Resources and Technical Services Division, American Library Association, on the recommendation of the Cataloging of Children's Materials Committee. Many of these headings have been incorporated into the *Sears List of Subject Headings*, 11th edition. The application of Library of Congress *Subject Headings for Children's Literature* enables a media centre to use the subject headings from Library of Congress copy and MARC tapes without alteration.

Although it is not widely used at this time, PRECIS (Preserved Context Index System) has won acceptance in some media centres since the publication of the PRECIS manual in 1974.

B. Media Form Subdivisions

Guidelines for the Subject Analysis of Audiovisual Materials (see Appendix C, page 127) suggests media form subdivisions, e.g. Batik — Motion pictures, as an optional addition to a subject heading. The use of such subdivisions depends on the size of the collection or the type of automated system.

Advantage:

In a long sequence of items listed under one heading, items in a particular format may not be found readily. If a media centre has requests which link subject matter to format, subdividing the sequence may make such information more accessible.

Disadvantages:

1. The segregation of items in the catalogue into format groupings erodes the concept of an integrated collection.
2. If both a general material designation and a medium form subdivision are listed in the record, the same information is given twice. This increases costs and is unnecessary in some automated systems. The terminology used for media form subdivisions is the same as that in the list of general material designations (see Appendix B, page 126).

C. Classification or Accession Number for Information Retrieval

The use of the same classification scheme for all media centre materials is suggested for the following reasons:

1. Media centre patrons find it easier to become acquainted with and use one system.
2. Wherever possible, materials on the same subject are stored together.
3. Emphasis is placed on content rather than form.
4. Centralized cataloguing and processing services do not assign non-standard call numbers, e.g., accession numbers.
5. Computer produced all-media bibliographies can be made available easily from the catalogue data.

Classifying materials for integrated collections necessitates flexible storage and the use of trained personnel. If constrictions on space and/or staff time make classification or intershelving difficult, materials can be organized by accession number. It is important to note that storage by accession number has the following drawbacks:

1. Materials on the same subject are not housed together because there is no relationship between call number and subject matter.
2. Added copies of a particular item may have different call numbers and be stored in different places.
3. The only subject approach to materials is through the catalogue.
4. Call numbers must be assigned by individual resource centres, thereby diminishing the economy of centralized services.

D. Classification

The media specialist should choose a classification scheme which is comprehensive, continuously revised, and proven in day-to-day use. The selection of a particular scheme is based generally on the anticipated size of the collection and the degree of specificity required in classification. The schemes used most commonly by certain types of media centres are mentioned below.

Many academic and research libraries are using the Library of Congress classification or the unabridged Dewey Decimal classification. Special libraries devoted to specific disciplines may use subject-oriented classification schemes, e.g., National Library of Medicine classification for health science collections.

Public libraries and many secondary school media centres report the use of the unabridged Dewey Decimal classification to the second and third prime marks, depending on the anticipated size of the collection. Libraries with small collections use the abridged Dewey, but keep in mind their plans for expansion and the possibility of future incorporation into a larger system.

Juvenile collections in elementary school media centres and public libraries are for the most part classified by the abridged Dewey Decimal classification, although the unabridged Dewey has been used successfully at this level.

Collections which are not organized for browsing may be shelved by some other scheme. However, if a classification scheme is not to be used immediately, the assignment of a classification number at the time the material is in the cataloguing department can be worthwhile. Shelving policies may change. In addition, many media centres with computers have enjoyed the benefit of being able to use a classification scheme to produce subject bibliographies and lists.

E. Call Letters, Identification Numbers

The decision whether to use call letters or specific numbering systems, e.g., Cutter numbers, will generally depend on the size of the collection or the type of automated system under consideration. Three call letters are usually sufficient to identify a particular item in a school media centre or a small-to-medium public library collection. Larger collections may require the use of specific identification numbers to assign a unique call number to each item.

Unique call numbers are important in some automated circulation systems, and such numbers used in conjunction with copy numbers can eliminate the expense of assigning accession numbers for exact identification.

F. Special Aspects of Subject Analysis for Nonbook Materials

The following concerns have been expressed about the subject analysis of nonbook materials by librarians, cataloguers, and media specialists.

1. *Precision of subject headings.* Some items need precise subject headings because:
    a) some media are not browsed easily
    b) the subject content of some media is very specific.
    Subject headings from standard lists are too general, in many instances, to identify precisely the subject content. There is no index, nor any quick way for the patron to browse the item, unless the producer has provided a good manual.

2. *Currency in subject analysis.* New subject matter may appear first in a nonbook format. Videotapes can create instant new subject content; sound tapes can capture a new idea long before it can be produced in book form. Due to administrative complexities, it is difficult to keep subject heading lists and classification systems current.

3. *Book orientation in subject headings and subdivisions.* It is misleading to apply "Laboratory manuals," "Counting books," "Conversation and phrase books," etc., to nonbook materials. The book-oriented wording should be rephrased so that appropriate subject headings can be used with all materials.

    Classification schemes and subject heading systems are constructed primarily for books; subject matter not commonly found in book format may not be included.

4. *Subject analysis for music recordings.* Cataloguers in public, school, and college libraries have found the classification and subject heading systems in the classical music field to be too academic for the unsophisticated patron and inadequate in their coverage of popular music.

5. *Subject analysis for motion pictures.* The popularity of film courses has resulted in patrons asking for motion pictures other than by subject matter. Librarians and media specialists would like headings for mood, technique, and genre, and classification for animated and experimental films.

Some of these concerns have been solved and others are under consideration. *Sears List of Subject Headings,* 11th edition, has, with a few exceptions, eliminated its book oriented headings.

It provides guidance to the cataloguing of nonbook materials and to the creation of new headings in its "Principles of the Sears list."

Quarterly cumulations of the *Library of Congress Subject Headings* are available on microform. Each quarterly microform is a completely new edition including all headings and references in the 8th edition and all subsequent additions and changes through the quarter of publication. These cumulations make new headings and changing terminology more readily available at a lower cost than was possible with the paper supplements.

Despite their best intentions it is impossible for the people who maintain the subject analysis systems mentioned above to anticipate needs generated by the information explosion and changing terminology. The cataloguer will face the necessity of using subject headings not found in standard lists. This must be done carefully if a media centre is to minimize recataloguing when standard lists are updated. The following suggestions might be considered:

1. Check other sources of cataloguing information, such as:
   a) Catalogues of recently published works, e.g., *Weekly Record, American Book Publisher's Record, Booklist, Quill and Quire*, for items which have similar subject content;
   b) The *Hennepin County Library Cataloging Bulletin* and the *Hennepin County Library Authority Files*, both of which are available at a reasonable cost and which are cognizant of the subject analysis of nonbook materials;
   c) Periodical indexes for items which have similar subject content, e.g., *Reader's Guide to Periodical Literature, Canadian Periodical Index, British Humanities Index*.
2. Use established patterns in the construction of subject headings. Check the media centre's catalogue and the latest editions or supplements of standard subject lists for similar headings and those on related topics.
3. The work itself may provide appropriate terminology. However, terms which are colloquial or faddish should be avoided.

The editors of all the major subject analysis systems welcome suggestions. Write to them about problem areas.

Media centres with collections devoted to specific disciplines, and which find the subject analysis schemes mentioned above inadequate, may wish to use the resources of the Subject Analysis Systems, Faculty of Library Science Library, University of Toronto (Room 404, 140 St. George St., Toronto, Ontario, Canada M5S 1A1). This collection of classification schemes, thesauri, and subject heading lists, which was housed previously in Case Western Reserve University School of Library Science, is the largest of its kind in North America. It is available for free use in the library or on interloan for a fee.

III.   METHODS OF INDICATING TYPE OF MATERIAL

A.   Colour-coding
Colour-coding is not recommended for the following reasons:

1. Photoreproduction of catalogue data is impractical because the use of colour film raises costs.
2. Colour-coding is also impractical for computer-produced book, microform, or online catalogues.
3. To make colour-coding economically feasible in centralized cataloguing, an internationally accepted standardized colour code would have to be established. At present there is no such standardization. Individual resource centres using such services would have to colour-code by hand, a time-consuming task.
4. As new types of media are acquired, the media centre would soon run out of distinctive colours. Shadings of colours could lead to confusion if the quality of colour were not maintained.
5. Colour-coding erodes the all-media approach to resource centre materials.

B.   Media Code as Part of the Call Number[1]
The use of a media code is not recommended. A media code used as an integral part of the call number has proved to be unsatisfactory in field tests. This type of call number caused individual items to be stored by medium, and the segregated shelving of items by medium resulted in an uneconomic use of space, since many items in a particular medium are produced or packaged in widely divergent sizes. A wiser use of storage space was made when the media code was abandoned and all media were intershelved. Oversized materials were then treated in the same manner as oversized books.

Despite the use of signs it was also found that patrons needed help from media centre staff to understand the media code. If public service and/or self service is the goal, a media centre will not complicate the call number by making it more mysterious than it already is.

A media code does not identify a medium as clearly as the more accurate general material designations (see below). Since a media code is not an effective agent for storage or medium identification, its use as an integral part of the call number should be discouraged.

If their size permits intershelving, all items should be stored by one classification scheme. Any item which can be housed with other media does not need an additional notation on the catalogue record. If an item cannot be intershelved in its proper place in the classification scheme, its location should be stated on the catalogue record in accordance with the method adopted for reference and oversize books.

C.   General Material Designations (formerly media designations)

A generic general material designation is listed in square brackets following the title proper. It is given early in the record to inform the user succinctly and immediately about the general format of the particular item. Users interested in this type of material will be prepared to read further in the physical description and note area for more detail. Users not wanting this general format may move quickly to the next listing.

The *Anglo-American Cataloguing Rules*, 2nd edition, provides options which can be applied to the use of general material designations. The advantages of each option are discussed below.

Option 1: General material designations are not used in the catalogue record.

Advantages:
a)   A truly integrated approach to the all-media catalogue;
b)   A solution to the terminology controversy which has raged since the first attempts were made to standardize media designations.

Disadvantages:
a)   Patrons will have to read the catalogue record more thoroughly than is commonly the case;
b)   Format will not be indicated in abbreviated entries, such as those in on-line catalogues and indexes to COM catalogues.

Option 2: General material designations are used in the catalogue record.

There are two official general material designation lists (see Appendix B, page 126) in the *Anglo-American Cataloguing Rules*, 2nd edition, which directs North American media centres to use the North American list, United Kingdom centres the British list. A third international standard list of general material designations may be found in the several volumes of rules for the International Standard Bibliographic Descriptions (ISBD).

Advantage:
An early warning signal alerts the patron about the format of an item.

Disadvantage:
No list of terms can find complete acceptance among its users. Some terms will be ambiguous to certain sectors of the public and/or certain geographical areas.

Careful consideration should be given to the implications of each of these alternatives.

A general material designation should be applied to all materials in the following types of media centres:
a)   Those who believe that their patrons will be frustrated by the lack of an early warning signal in the catalogue record;
b)   Those with abbreviated record on-line or COM catalogues;
c)   Those with indexes to COM catalogues.

Some communications received by the authors have pointed strongly to the importance of applying general material designations to book as well as nonbook materials. Indeed, it seems unreasonable to give a general material designation to a radio speech on cassette but not to the same thing produced in a booklet, or in many cases, on microform. The application of a general material designation to every item will make the catalogue much more intelligible to the average patron.

The North American list of general material designations is used in this book. Those electing option 1 or the British list in option 2 or the ISBD list may use the rules on the following pages by disregarding the general material designation or by substituting the appropriate term from the British or ISBD lists.

A generic term is used to avoid the proliferation of general material designations which may develop if specific designations are used. It is anticipated that the list of general material designations shown below will be hospitable to new media in the future. In addition, generic general material designations will allow a resource centre to produce a basic record which can be used for works reproduced in various formats of the same medium (see sample cards 79, 109, 124).

The list of general material designations below is limited to those formats which are discussed in this book. For a complete list of general material designations see Appendix B, page 126 .

Art original
Chart
Diorama
Filmstrip
Flash card
Game
Globe
Kit
Machine-readable data file
Map
Microform
Microscope slide
Model
Motion picture
Picture

Realia
Slide
Sound recording
Technical drawing
Transparency
Videorecording

Laboratory kits and programmed learning packages are catalogued under the general material designation which best describes the item. Laboratory kits consisting of many textual parts are catalogued as ''kit.''

An architectural rendering is catalogued under ''art original'' or ''picture'' depending on whether it is the original drawing or a reproduction.

Specific terms may be necessary in a specialized collection. It is advisable, however, for such a collection to keep its list of designations as generic as possible.

Definitions of the media included in the above designations are given in the glossary on pages 109 to 110.

General Information Concerning Sample Cards and the Three Levels of Cataloguing

Throughout this book the catalogue card is used to illustrate cataloguing rules because it makes the samples easily identifiable. One card format is used for consistency. There is no standard format used by all media centres, nor do all catalogues exist in card form. There are many book catalogues and an increasing number of COM and on-line catalogues. The format applied to cataloguing the resource centre's book collection should be used for all materials.

The Anglo-American Cataloguing Rules, 2nd edition, recommends three levels of detail in description and prescribes the minimum set of elements to be included at each level. Additional elements may be listed if the cataloguer considers such information important.

FIRST LEVEL OF DESCRIPTION

The minimum elements required at this level include:

> title proper
> general material designation[2]
> first statement of responsibility, if different from main entry heading or if item has a title main entry
> edition statement
> mathematical data or material specific details (for cartographic materials and serial publications only)
> first publisher/producer
> date of publication/production
> extent of item
> note(s)
> standard number

Elementary school media centres, children's libraries, centres where the patron's needs are not sophisticated, and small collections without large growth potential or where limited staff makes detailed cataloguing impractical are likely to adopt the first level of description. Throughout this book Sears subject headings, abridged Dewey Decimal classification, and author letters are assigned to first level descriptive cataloguing.

SECOND LEVEL OF DESCRIPTION

The minimum elements required at this level include:

> title proper
> general material designation
> parallel title and other title information
> first statement of responsibility and other statements of responsibility
> edition statement and first statement of responsibility relating to the edition
> mathematical data or material specific details (for cartographic materials and serial publications only)
> first place of publication/production and, if applicable, place in the country of the cataloguing agency
> first publisher/producer and, if applicable, publisher/producer in the country of the cataloguing agency
> date of publication/production
> extent of item
> other physical details
> dimensions
> series statement (title proper of series, statement of responsibility relating to series, ISSN, numbering within series, title of subseries, ISSN of subseries, numbering within subseries)
> note(s)
> standard number

The majority of media centres will probably adopt the second level of description. Library of Congress subject headings, unabridged Dewey Decimal classification and Cutter numbers are given to items with second level descriptions in this book.

THIRD LEVEL OF DESCRIPTION

All elements are required at this level.

The third level of description is intended for national libraries, research libraries, and those with a need for detailed cataloguing information. In this book Library of Congress classification and subject headings are given to items catalogued at the third level.

In all levels *A List of Canadian Subject Headings* or *Sears List of Subject Headings: Canadian Companion* are used, if applicable.

Sample cards 1,2 and 3 demonstrate the three levels of description applied to the same item. The sample cards in each section contain items catalogued at the three levels, and the terms "1st level," "2nd level," and "3rd level" are listed on the line underneath the sample card number. Because the authors anticipate the use of first or second level cataloguing by most media centres, there are fewer third level examples than first and second level.

In each section there are sample cards with "compare with NBM/1 s.c. ——" noted in the margin. This cryptic notation means "compare with *Nonbook Materials*, 1st edition, sample card ——." At least one item from each section of the previous edition of this book has been selected for recataloguing to highlight the recent rule changes.

Furthermore, the recatalogued samples have been placed in different levels of description. In some instances the subject headings and/or call numbers assigned to a particular item in NBM/1 will be different in this book because the level of description chosen for the item has dictated a different subject analysis system (see above paragraphs). The new edition of *Sears List of Subject Headings* has also caused some changes.

Please note that the Library of Congress classification numbers vary in specificity to demonstrate a variety of call numbers. This has also been done with the call letters in 1st level cataloguing. There are also variations in the tracing. For example, sample cards 67, 71, and 105 demonstrate the addition of a general material designation to an added entry. This designation would be added if a media centre wishes to segregate formats in its file.

The sample cards as a whole have been chosen to illustrate the most frequently used cataloguing rules. However, those in the sections on Filmstrips and Kits have been specially marked to demonstrate the basic rules to students and other inexperienced cataloguers.

Sample card 1
1st level

370.11	Skeel, Dorothy J.
SKE	Developing creative ability [sound recording]. -- H. Wilson, c1974.
	2 cassettes (ca. 20 min.)

1. Creative ability.   2. Speech.   I. Title.

370.118 Skeel, Dorothy J.
Sk23   Developing creative ability [sound recording] / Dorothy J.
         Skeel ; editors, E.L. Richardson and James H. Cole. -- South
         Holland, Ill. : H. Wilson, c1974.
             2 sound cassettes (ca. 20 min.) : 3³/₄ ips, mono. + 1
         descriptive sheet. -- (Language arts ; LI-CT)

             Intended audience: K-6.
             Contents: Listening fun -- Activities for creative writing --
         Using descriptive words -- Sound stories.

             1. Creative ability.   2. Speech.   I. Title.

BF   Skeel, Dorothy J.
408   Developing creative ability [sound recording] / Dorothy J.
S54   Skeel ; editors, E.L. Richardson and James H. Cole. -- South
         Holland, Ill. : H. Wilson [producer] ; Chicago : Encyclopaedia
         Britannica [distributor], c1974.
             2 sound cassettes (ca. 20 min.) : 3³/₄ ips, mono. + 1
         descriptive sheet (2 p. ; 23 cm.). -- (Language arts ; LI-CT)

             Subtitle on descriptive sheet: Listening, writing, oral
         interpretation and dramatic activities.

                                              (Continued on next card)

BF   Skeel, Dorothy J. -- Developing creative ability [sound recording]
408   ... c1974. (Card 2)
S54
             Reissue of 1967 work.
             Series no. on container: LI; on descriptive sheet LI-T.
             Intended audience: K-6.
             Contents: Listening fun -- Activities for creative writing --
         Using descriptive words -- Sound stories.

             1. Creative ability.   2. Speech.   I. Title.

Cataloguing Rules for Nonbook Materials

2

General Rules for Entry and Descriptive Cataloguing

The Anglo-American Cataloguing Rules, 2nd edition, prescribes the same rules of entry and description for all materials. The following rules are those which will be applied to nonbook materials most frequently. Exceptions to these rules are dictated by the nature of a particular medium and will be discussed under the medium heading.

All items must be examined by the cataloguer and should be screened or played to ensure accuracy of bibliographic information.

SOURCES OF INFORMATION

Cataloguing information for the title and statement of responsibility area, the edition area, the publication/distribution, etc. area, and the series area should be taken from the following sources in the order indicated:

1. The material itself, including the container when it is an integral part of an item, e.g., a cassette (chief source of information). If there is more than one title on the material, precedence is given to the one positioned closest to the physical content;[3]
2. Accompanying data, e.g., manuals, sheets, etc., issued with the item;
3. The container, where it is not an integral or unifying part of the item (see 1 above) and, therefore, may be discarded;
4. Outside sources, such as bibliographies, producer's brochures, etc. If the source of the information is not stated in the note area, the information is enclosed in square brackets;
5. Information supplied by the cataloguer. Such information is enclosed in square brackets. Supplied titles should be descriptive, reasonably concise, and if possible begin with a filing word which reflects subject content.

If an item consists of more than one part, the chief source of information is as follows:

1. The piece that could be considered "the first part." In nonbook terms this might be the part which gives meaning to the various parts,[4] e.g., a manual or a container which is the unifying element;[5]

2. The part which gives the most information;
3. The container.

The chief source of information is identified in most of the sections of this book dealing with a specific medium. It is from this source that the title and statements of responsibility are taken. If the title must be taken from another part of the item, either because the chief source has no title or another part of the item has the most complete information, the source of the title is given in the note area. Dioramas, games, microscope slides, models, and realia are exceptions to this because the item, accompanying materials, and container are all considered chief sources of information.

There are no particular sources of information for the material specific details area, the physical description area, the note area, and the standard number and terms of availability area. Information for these areas can be drawn from any source.

ORGANIZATION AND PUNCTUATION OF THE DESCRIPTIVE CATALOGUING

The descriptive cataloguing is divided into 8 areas:

> title and statement of responsibility area
> edition area
> mathematical data or material specific details area (used only for cartographic materials or serials)
> publication, distribution, etc. area
> physical description area
> series area
> note area
> standard number and terms of availability area

Except where paragraphing is used, each of these areas is separated by a period-space-dash-space (. —). Internal punctuation for each of these areas is described below.

MAIN ENTRY

Entry under title will occur more frequently for nonbook than book materials because authorship cannot be established as readily for many nonbook items.

The following rules of main entry are to be applied in the order in which they are listed.

1. A reproduction of a work originally produced in another medium is entered in the same manner as the original work.
2. A work for which authorship can be clearly established is entered under author. The *Anglo-American Cataloguing Rules*, 2nd edition, defines author as "the person chiefly responsible for the creation of the intellectual or artistic content of a work. For example, ... composers of music are the authors of the works they create ... cartographers are the authors of their maps; and artists and photographers are the authors of the works they create." Authorship is not normally attributed to consultants, performers, producers, directors, designers, etc. (See 3 below for exceptions.)
3. A sound recording, motion picture, or videorecording in which the responsibility of the performing group goes beyond that of performance is entered under the performing group.
4. An item without a collective title is entered under the heading appropriate to the first work. (See pages 80 to 82 for rules for sound recordings without a collective title.)
5. A work for which authorship cannot be established because of the extent and nature of collaborative authorship is entered under title.

See page 80 for rules which allow entry under performer for sound recordings with and without a collective title.

TITLE AND STATEMENT OF RESPONSIBILITY AREA

The following will provide guidance for the cataloguing of many nonbook items. When these brief rules will not suffice, see The *Anglo-American Cataloguing Rules*, 2nd edition, rule 1.1.

Title proper
The title proper (formerly called the short title) is copied exactly from the chief source of information. However, capitalization and punctuation follow prescribed rules. A lengthy title may be shortened after 5 words by the marks of omission if clarity is not sacrificed.

General material designation
A discussion of general material designations will be found on pages 9 to 10. A general material designation is listed in lower case letters, in the singular, and in its own square brackets immediately following the title proper.

An exception to the placement and bracketing of the general material designation is made for items which are catalogued with a uniform title. The cataloguer has the option of placing a general material designation after the uniform title, capitalized and separated from the uniform title by a period and one space (.). If the uniform title is enclosed in square brackets, the general material designation is included in these brackets. See page 19 for the placement of the general material designation on records for items without a collective title.

Select the general material designation for the format, not for the content. For example, a map on a transparency is designated "transparency" rather than "map."

Occasionally a media centre receives an item which could be used in more than one way. The general material designation chosen should reflect its probable use. If probable use includes more than one general material designation category, regard it as a laboratory kit and apply the designation "kit."[6] (See sample cards 22 and 35.)

See page 10 and Appendix B for the list of general material designations.

Parallel titles and Other title information
Parallel titles are listed after the general material designation. Other title information also follows the general material designation and the title proper or parallel title to which it pertains. Both are listed in the exact wording found in the chief source of information. Lengthy other title information can be shortened after five words by the marks of omission if clarity is not sacrificed. Alternatively, lengthy other title information can be given in a note.

> *Punctuation*. A parallel title is separated from the title proper by a space-equal sign-space (=); the other title information is separated from the title proper or the parallel title by a space-colon-space (:). The general material designation is enclosed in its own set of square brackets.

Statements of responsibility
The statement(s) of responsibility is listed wherever possible in the wording and order found on the source(s) of information. Minor variations may be made to maintain grammatical clarity. A word or phrase may be added in square brackets in order to clarify the type of responsibility. (See sample card 117.)

Statements of responsibility may include authors, illustrators, translators, editors, directors, producers, performers, etc. — any person or corporate body which has contributed to the intellectual or artistic content. Contributors of minor importance may be listed in the notes. (See pages 64 and 81 for more specific rules about the statement of responsibility.)

There are many instances in nonbook materials where it is difficult to establish clear responsibility. For example, the item described on sample card 67 gives no indication that Jack Megenity did anything more than write the accompanying notes or that the Ideal School Supply Company had any responsibility other than that of manufacture and sale. When there is doubt concerning the responsibility for the artistic and/or intellectual content of the item, it is wiser to omit the statement than to construct one of dubious truth.[7]

In first level cataloguing the statement of responsibility is omitted only if it repeats the main entry heading, and statements of subsidiary responsibility (illustrators, editors, translators, directors, etc.) are given only if their names would be important to the media centre's patrons and, therefore, traced.

Punctuation. The statement of responsibility is separated from the title by a space-slash-space (/). Each type of responsibility is separated by a space-semicolon-space (;), e.g., / written by Jane Brown and John Black ; illustrated by Thomas Green and Mary White.

Items without a collective title

Items without a collective title may be described in one of the following ways:

1. If one work is clearly predominant, catalogue it and list the other works in a note (see sample card 130).
2. If no work is predominant, list the titles (and statements of responsibility, if works are by different authors) in the order in which they appear in the chief source of information (see sample cards 101, 110, 122). The general material designation is listed immediately after the last of a group of titles by one author. If an item has works by different authors, the general material designation is listed after the last statement of responsibility. See page 18 for the placement of a general material designation used with a uniform title.

Punctuation. If the works are all by the same author(s), the individual titles are separated by space-semicolon-space (;). If the works are by different authors, the title and statement of responsibility area for each work is separated from the one previously listed by a period and 2 spaces (.   ).

3. Make a separate description[8] for each part that has a distinctive title, and link the descriptions in a "with" note (see sample cards 56, 102A, 102B, 123A, 123B). This method is most useful when the separate items have quite different subject headings.
4. Supply a collective title[9] and state the reason and/or source of the supplied title in a note (see sample card 72). This method is most useful when there is a large number of parts or when the parts have separate titles which are non-distinctive, e.g., "Introduction," "Agriculture," "Geography," etc.

EDITION AREA

The edition statement is listed as it appears on the item, using arabic numerals and standard abbreviations.

A statement of responsibility relating to a particular edition is listed following the edition statement and is separated from it by a space-slash-space (/).

MATHEMATICAL DATA OR MATERIAL SPECIFIC DETAILS AREA

This area is used only with cartographic materials and serials in the sections on globes, maps, and microforms.

PUBLICATION, DISTRIBUTION, ETC., AREA

Place

List the name of the place as it appears on the item and add the name of the province, state, country, etc., if it is necessary for identification.

When more than one place appears on the item, list in the following order:

the first named place, and
the most prominently named place, if different from the first named place, and
the first named place in the country of the cataloguing agency, if different from the first two.

If no probable place can be listed, give the name of the province, state, country, etc.

If the place is unknown, list "S.1." in square brackets.

Publisher, distributor, etc.

List the name of the publisher, producer, distributor, etc., in the shortest form that can be identified internationally.

A publisher, etc., who has appeared in the title and statement of responsibility area is listed in an abbreviated form.

When more than one publisher appears on the item, list place and corresponding publisher in the following order:

> the first named place and publisher, and
> the most prominently named place and publisher, if different from the first named, and
> the first named place and publisher in the country of the cataloguing agency, if different from the first two.

If the bodies named perform different functions, e.g., producer and distributor, both are listed.

> *Option*. List a statement of function following the name of the distributor, publisher, producer, or production company (see sample cards 12, 73, 76, 78, 79, etc.).

If the publisher, etc. is unknown, list "s.n." in square brackets and follow this by the place and name of the manufacturer if this information is given on the item.

Date

List the publication date of the item being catalogued. If the date of distribution or release is different and considered significant, list it also.

> *Option*. If the latest copyright date is different, list it following the publication/distribution date.

If the dates of publication or distribution cannot be ascertained, list the copyright date, or failing that, the date of manufacture.

If no date can be found, give an approximate date. (See the *Anglo-American Cataloguing Rules*, 2nd edition, rule 1.4F7.)

> *Option*. If the information is considered important, the place, name of manufacturer, and/or

date of manufacture may be added in parentheses at the end of the publication, distribution, etc. area.

Punctuation. Place is separated from a second place by a space-semicolon-space (;) and from a publisher or manufacturer by a space-colon-space (:).

A publisher or manufacturer is separated from a date by a comma and one space (,).

A place and publisher are separated from a second place and publisher by a space-semicolon-space (;).

The place, name, and date of manufacture are enclosed in parentheses.

PHYSICAL DESCRIPTION AREA (Previously named COLLATION)

The information to be listed in this area is detailed in the rules for each medium. General points are discussed below.

Extent of item

The *number of physical units* in the item being catalogued is recorded in arabic numerals, together with a specific material designation, e.g., 6 study prints, 2 microfiches.

In some cases, the number of *components* is listed in parentheses after the specific material designation, e.g., 1 transparency (4 overlays). If the components are too numerous to count, an approximate figure may be listed, e.g., 1 filmstrip (ca. 90 fr.) or the term "various pieces" used, e.g., 1 diorama (various pieces).

When appropriate, the *playing time* is listed in parentheses after the specific material designation. Playing time is given in minutes, with parts of minutes being taken to the next minute. If playing time is less than 5 minutes, it is listed in minutes and seconds.

> *Option*.[10] If the general material designation and the specific material designation are the same, the specific material designation can be omitted (see sample cards 10, 13, 14, 15, etc.).

> *Option*. If the specific material designation contains words or prefixes the same as those found in the general material designation, those words or prefixes can be omitted (see sample cards 21, 22, 53, etc.).

Other physical details

The nature of each medium dictates the information to be listed as other physical details. It may include sound, colour, process or method of reproduction, mounting, material, projection, playing speed, track information, etc. Specific instructions are given with the rules for each medium.

Punctuation. The statement of other physical details is preceded by a space-colon-space (:).

Dimensions

Two-dimensional media are measured height × width, three-dimensional materials height × width × depth. Fractions are taken to the next number. If the parts of an item have varying sizes, the largest measurement is given followed by the phrase "or smaller."[11] If the outer dimensions of the parts are the same, but some of the parts are designed to be viewed horizontally and some vertically, give the measurement of the majority as the measurements of the set.[12]

If an item is housed in a container, the type of container may be listed together with its dimensions.[13]

The dimensions in the specific rules in this book are those required by the *Anglo-American Cataloguing Rules*, 2nd edition. Some are in metric numbers and some in inches. A media centre may decide to list all dimensions in metric measurement.

Punctuation. The statement of dimensions is preceded by a space-semicolon-space (;).

Accompanying material

If an item contains two or more media, one of which is clearly predominant, it is catalogued by the dominant medium and the subordinate accompanying material may be listed after the dimensions. When accompanying material is promotional in nature and of limited value, it need not be listed.

If an item has more than one accompanying material, this information is given as for example, + 2 charts + 1 teacher's guide.[14]

Option. Other physical details and dimensions may be added.

If information about the accompanying material cannot be given succinctly, the accompanying material is not listed at the end of the physical description area; it is given in the note area (see sample cards 9, 14, 16, etc.).

See also page 40 for a discussion of items which contain different types of materials.

Punctuation. The statement of accompanying material is preceded by a space-plus sign-space (+). Details of accompanying material are placed in parentheses.

SERIES AREA

If applicable, a series statement in parentheses follows the physical description area. The series area in 3rd level cataloguing could include:

title proper of series
parallel titles
other title information
statements of responsibility
International Standard Serial Number (ISSN)
numbering within series
subseries and its parallel titles, other title information, and statement of responsibility
ISSN of subseries
numbering of subseries

If an item belongs to two or more series rather than a series and subseries, each series is enclosed within its own parentheses.

Those who elect 2nd level description will develop a policy for the amount of detail to be given in the series area.

Series may be omitted in 1st level cataloguing. However, series to be traced and those which add substantially to an understanding of the catalogue record should be listed.

NOTE AREA

All notes are optional. 1st level cataloguing should list notes which are essential to the use of the item. Those who elect 2nd level cataloguing will develop a policy for notes useful to their institutions. 3rd level cataloguing notes will be the most detailed.

In the rules for specific media in this book, only notes of particular importance to the medium are listed.

If for some reason a piece of information which has been prescribed for some area of the descriptive cataloguing cannot be listed in its proper place, it is listed in the note area. An example of this is sample card 68. The statement of colour has been omitted from the physical description area because an accurate description of colour could not be given concisely. The item was received uncoloured from the producer and the user is instructed to colour and wash the model as necessary.

Other information which may be given in notes is listed in the following order:

Nature, scope, or artistic form

Language, translation, and/or adaptation

Source of title proper

Variations in title

Parallel titles and other title information (if not listed in the title and statement of responsibility area)

Statements of responsibility. This may include additional information (e.g., performers) not listed in the title and statement of responsibility area or statements of responsibility not taken from the chief source of information (see sample card 36)

Edition and history

Material specific details such as mathematical and other cartographic data

Additional information about publication, distribution, etc.

Additional information concerning the physical description, particularly if such information affects the item's use. The authors have followed the example used in the *Anglo-American Cataloguing Rules*, 2nd edition, rule 11.7B10 for listing equipment necessary for the effective use of an item (see sample cards 19, 59, 114, 121). However, a system can be programmed to provide a listing of all materials in a collection requiring special equipment if the note is given in the following manner — "For use with :" (see sample card 33)

Accompanying materials and supplements (if not listed elsewhere)

Additional information about series

Audience level as stated on the item is listed. Such information may not be desirable in a public catalogue, particularly for juvenile and youth collections

Other formats available. This note is used by (1) large bibliographic agencies whose cataloguing records are used by other than their own patrons, (2) individual media centres which have more than one format of an item catalogued under the same general material designation and which have chosen to list all formats on the same card (see sample cards 79, 109, 124)

Summaries. These are not necessary for media which can be readily examined or adequately described by title and/or series statement. However such items as motion pictures or videorecordings usually require description in a summary. A summary should describe subject content succinctly and objectively without evaluation. If clarity can be maintained, words and phrases may be substituted for sentences.

Contents

Numbers associated with item other than ISBNs or ISSNs (see below)

Peculiarities of the particular copy the media centre holds and the media centre's holdings if the item is incomplete

"With" notes are used when an item has separately titled parts and no collective title

Punctuation. Each note is preceded by a period-space-dash-space (. —) or is placed in its own paragraph. Introductory words, such as Summary or Contents, are separated from the content of their paragraphs by a colon-space (:).

STANDARD NUMBER AND TERMS OF AVAILABILITY AREA

List the ISBN (International Standard Book Number) or ISSN (International Standard Serial Number) or any other internationally recognized standard number.

If two such numbers appear on the item, list the one that applies to the item being catalogued. In a multipart item list the one that applies to the whole item (see sample card 91).

The key-title of a serial follows the ISSN. Do not list the key-title if no ISSN is found.

Option. Terms of availability are listed if known.

If there are two standard numbers, a brief qualification follows each number. Special terms of availability are also qualified.

Punctuation. A standard number is separated from a key-title by a space-equal sign-space (=). Qualifications are enclosed in parentheses. The terms of availability are preceded by a space-colon-space (:).

Art Originals[15]

Art original: an original two- or three-dimensional work of art.

Original paintings, drawings, architectural renderings, and sculpture are included under this heading and designated by the term "art original." Art prints, two-dimensional art reproductions, photographs, and reproductions of architectural renderings are designated "picture" (see page 71). Three-dimensional art reproductions are designated "model" (see page 62).

The general rules on pages 17 to 22 apply with the following additions and exceptions.

Sources of information[16]
Information for the catalogue record is taken from the following sources in this order:

1. The item itself;
2. Frame or mount;
3. Accompanying material;
4. Other sources.

Publication, distribution, etc. area
List only the date of creation.

Physical description area
Extent of item. List the number of art originals.

Option. If the general material designation "art original" is used, a specific term may be listed (see sample card 5).

Other physical details. List materials used, e.g., oil on canvas.

Dimensions. For two-dimensional items, height × width of the item itself excluding mount or frame are listed in centimetres. For three-dimensional items height × width × depth or a single dimension with a word or phrase identifying the dimension are listed in centimetres.

Note area
List the nature of the item unless this is apparent from the rest of the catalogue record (see sample card 4).

Information about mounting or framing is given if such information affects the use of the item.

Subject analysis
Call numbers have been assigned to the following sample cards even though original works of art are not likely to be intershelved due to their fragility and possible value. Numbers are often required for circulation and shelf listing purposes.

The expected use of the item will determine subject headings. Those assigned to the following items demonstrate possible subject headings. If a media centre has patrons who ask, for example, for sculptures of seals then "Seals (Animals) — Sculpture" would be added to sample card 5.

Levels of description
The majority of media centres with multimedia collections will not possess well known, valuable works of art. Therefore, items will need to be identified with some precision. (Are there other paintings by Christie which he has named "Untitled" and given a precise date? A first level description may not be useful in this case.) It is recommended that the catalogue record for works of art be as full as possible.

Care, handling, and storage
See General Guidelines for the Care, Handling, and Storage of Two-Dimensional, Opaque Materials on page 118 and General Guidelines for the Storage of Three-Dimensional Media on page 118.

The care of valuable items requires more guidance than is given in this book.

```
ND        Christie, Robert.
245           Untitled [art original] / Christie. -- 1972.
C497          1 art original : acrylic on paper ; 50 × 64 cm.
1972
              Abstract painting.
              Date on work: Apr. 24, 1972.
              Size when framed: 54 × 69 cm.



          1. Paintings, Canadian.
```

```
E         [Man with seal] [art original]. -- [19--]
99            1 sculpture : soapstone ; 23 cm. high.
E7
M35           Title supplied by cataloguer.
1900z         Only identifying mark: E-7-730.




          1. Eskimos - Sculpture.
```

Charts

Chart: a sheet of information arranged in tabular or graphic form produced on an opaque backing.

Charts, wall charts and flip charts are included under this heading and designated by the term "chart."

Charts may be organized as ephemeral materials, in a vertical file (see pages 103 to 105). Items of permanent value to the collection should be completely catalogued for their effective use.

The general rules on pages 17 to 22 apply with the following additions and exceptions.

Sources of information
The container is preferred to the accompanying data.

Physical description area
Extent of item. List the number of charts, flip charts, or wall charts.

> *Flip charts*. List in parentheses the number of sheets if opaque or the number of overlays if transparent.[17]

Other physical details. If appropriate, list double sides[18] (see sample card 9). List b&w or col.

Dimensions. Height × width are listed in centimetres. If appropriate, height × width when folded is listed also[19] (see sample card 9).

Care, handling, and storage
See General Guidelines for the Care, Handling, and Storage of Two-Dimensional, Opaque Materials on page 118.

595.7	Butterfly specimens [chart]. -- Taiwan : [s.n., 19--]
But	1 chart.

Captions in English, Chinese, Japanese.
Summary: 50 specimens with real wings and paper bodies mounted between 2 sheets of plastic.

1. Butterflies.

○

Sample card 6[20]
1st level

Country only given; place name, publisher/producer and date unknown

Sample card 7
1st level

```
529        Solar year wheel [chart]. -- Ideal School Supply, c1970.
Sol            1 wallchart.




           1. Calendars.   2. Seasons.   3. Time.
```

Wallchart

Sample card 8
2nd level

Compare with
NBM/1 s.c. 39

```
025.3      Bergwall, Charles.
B454v          Vicalog [chart] : Eye Gate visual card catalog / conceived and
           designed by Charles Bergwall and Sherwin S. Glassner. --
           Jamaica, N.Y. : Eye Gate, [196-?]
               1 flip chart (4 attached overlays) : b&w ; 23 × 35 cm.




               1. Catalogs, Card.   2. Cataloging.   I. Glassner, Sherwin S.
           II. Title.
```

Flip chart

Sample card 9[21]
3rd level

Accompanying
material listed
in note area; variant title
noted

```
QB         Nasca, Donald.
6              Astronomy - space [chart] / Donald Nasca ; designed by
N38        Charles Cary ; consultant, Mario E. Motter. -- Dansville, N.Y. :
1968       Instructor Publications, c1968.
               5 charts : double sides, col. ; 63 × 41 cm. folded to 31 ×
           41 cm. in descriptive case, 32 × 42 cm. -- (Science concepts and
           processes ; 589)

               Teachers guide (12 p.) titled: Astronomy and space.
```

(Continued on next card)

Sample card 9
(continued)

QB   Nasca, Donald. -- Astronomy - space [chart] ... c1968.   (Card 2)
6
N38   Contents: 1. Space. 6. Constellations -- 2. Solar system: sun.
1968   7. Telescope -- 3. Solar system: planets. 8. Navigation -- 4.
              Satellites. 9. Space flight -- 5. Comets and meteors. 10. Space
              exploration.

              1. Astronomy.   2. Outer space.   I. Title.

Dioramas

Diorama: a scene produced in three dimensions by placing objects, figures, etc., in front of a representational background.

The general rules on pages 17 to 22 apply with the following additions and exceptions.

Physical description area
Extent of item. List the number of dioramas and add in parentheses the number of pieces. When the number of pieces cannot be ascertained easily, the term "various pieces" is used.

Option. If the general material designation "diorama" is used, the term "1 diorama" may be omitted (see sample card 10).

Other physical details. List the material from which the item was made and col. or b&w, if such information is useful.

Dimensions. List the type of packaging and its dimensions.

Care, handling and storage
See General Guidelines for the Storage of Three-Dimensional Media on page 118.

Sample card 10
1st level

525   Seasons - fall and winter [diorama]. -- Instructo Products, c1966.
SEA   various pieces.

Compare with
NBM/1 s.c. 40

1. Autumn.   2. Winter.

792.   The Shakespearian stage [diorama]. -- London:
022   Unicorn Media, 1979.
Sh15   1 diorama (50 pieces) : col. ; in box, 25 × 25 × 6 cm. + 1
manual. -- (Theatre diorama series)

     1. Theaters - Stage setting and scenery.   I. Series.

SF   A Sheep farm in New Zealand [diorama] / Farm
375.5   Economics Section, Ministry of Agriculture and Fisheries. --
N45   Wellington : [s.n.] : Lomax [distributor], 1978.
S54   1 diorama (various pieces) : cardboard and plastic, col. ; in
1978   box, 36 × 24 × 16 cm.

     Contains 1 farm house, 3 barns, 100 sheep, 14 other animals,
9 people, assorted farm equipment, plan of a typical farm, cost
sheets, and other financial papers.
     Intended audience: Grades 6-10.

     (Continued on next card)

SF   A Sheep farm in New Zealand [diorama] ... 1978.   (Card 2)
375.5
N45   Summary: The economic management of a sheep farm can be
S54   demonstrated by the movement of the pieces.
1978

     1. Sheep ranches - New Zealand   I. New Zealand. Farm
Economics Section.

Filmstrips

Filmstrip: a roll of film containing a succession of images designed to be viewed one frame at a time. A short length of such film, sometimes mounted in rigid format, is called a filmslip.

Filmstrips and filmslips are included under this heading and designated by the term "filmstrip."

The general rules on pages 17 to 22 apply with the following additions and exceptions.

Sources of information

Information for the catalogue record is taken from the following sources in this order:

1. The item itself (chief source of information). Preference should be given to the information on the title frames rather than the leader frames.[22] Title frames immediately precede the main body of the filmstrip while the leader frames are separated from the body of the filmstrip by a length of blank film;
2. Container;
3. Accompanying material;
4. Other sources.

Physical description area

Extent of item. List the number of filmstrips, filmstrip cartridges, or filmslips and in parentheses the number of frames. The last numbered frame or, if applicable, the last numbered double frame, is recorded.[23] If the title frames are numbered separately, list both the number of content frames and the number of title or other frames. If the frames are unnumbered, one of the following methods is used to determine the number of frames.

1. The frames in an unnumbered filmstrip are counted and this information is added in square brackets,[24] e.g., [48] fr. The count should begin with the first content frame and end with the last content frame.[25]
2. If a media centre does not wish to spend time counting frames, it can use the following method, which will give a fairly accurate

approximation for single frame filmstrips. Measure from the first content frame to the last content frame. There are 16 frames to every foot (12 inches) of a 35 mm., single frame filmstrip, e.g., length = 50 inches; no. of frames = $50 \times 16/12 = 66.67$ which represents 67 frames. This is listed as ca. 67 fr. In metric measurement each 40 centimetres contains 21 frames, e.g., length = 87 centimetres; no. of frames = $87 \times 21/40 = 45.7$ which represents 46 frames. This is listed as ca. 46 fr.

Option. If a general material designation is used, the term "1 filmstrip" may be omitted (see sample cards, 13, 14, 16).

Other physical details. If the sound is integral, list it.
List b&w or col.

Dimensions. Width is listed in millimetres.

Note area

If the images in a double-frame filmstrip are placed such that a projector with a swivelling device must be used in order to utilize the filmstrip effectively, this information is noted, e.g., Images placed in frame horizontally and vertically.

If special equipment must be used to view a filmslip mounted in a rigid format, the equipment is noted (see sample card 33).

Care, handling, and storage

See General Guidelines for the Care, Handling, and Storage of Film Media on page 116.

The rapid development in methods of shelving filmstrips with other media make true intershelving possible. These shelving aids range from containers which simulate book binding to book ends containing filmstrip storage.

The sample cards for filmstrips demonstrate some of the common cataloguing principles which should be applied to all nonbook materials. These principles are noted to the right of the card.

		Sample card 13 1st level

025.3
BER
	Bergwall, Charles.
	    Introduction to the card catalog [filmstrip] / written by Charles
	Bergwall and Sherwin S. Glassner. -- Eye Gate, c1962.
	    35 fr. -- (Library services)
		Entry under
		author
		
		Compare with
		NBM/1 s.c. 43

	1. Catalogs, Card. I. Glassner, Sherwin S. II. Series.	Joint authors

		Sample card 14 1st level

709.32
FIV
	5,000 years of Egyptian art [filmstrip]. -- Educational Productions,
	    c1968.
	    28 double fr.
	
	    Notes by A.E. Halliwell.
		Compare with
		NBM/1 s.c. 44
		Entry under title
		Accompanying
		material listed in
		note area

	1. Art, Egyptian.	Double frames

		Sample card 15 2nd level

578.8
V277
	Vance, Adrian G.
	    Introduction to stem sectioning and staining [filmstrip] /
	author-photographer, Adrian G. Vance. -- Chicago : Society for
	Visual Education, 1962.
	    1 filmstrip ([37] fr.) : col. ; 35 mm. -- (The Microscope and
	its use ; 4)
	
	    Captions.
		Compare with
		NBM/1 s.c. 42

	1. Stains and staining (Microscopy). I. Series.	Unnumbered frames

301.45   Three nomadic peoples [filmstrip]. -- [Toronto] : Fitzhenry &
T413   Whiteside, c1973.
        24 fr. : col. ; 35 mm. -- (Man in his world filmstrip series.
Nomadic journey ; 1)

        Stored in a Bell and Howell autoload cartridge.
        Guide (7 p.) by John Parr.
        Summary: The life, habitat, and clothing of Bedouins, Eskimos,
and Lapps.

        1. Nomads.   2. Bedouins.   3. Eskimos.   4. Lapps.
I. Series.

Sample card 16[26]
2nd level

Subseries

Accompanying
material listed in
note area

Summary

---

428   Punctuation [filmstrip] / consultant, Edward F. Meany ; artist,
P969   Clyde V. Strohsahl. -- New York : Filmstrip House, c1961.
        4 filmstrips (ca. 27 fr. each) : col. ; 35 mm. -- (Language
arts)

        Captions.
        Contents: 1. Period, question mark, exclamation mark --
2. Comma, semicolon -- 3. Colon, dash, parentheses, quotation
marks -- 4. Examples and exercises.

        1. English language - Punctuation.

Sample card 17
2nd level

Number of
frames listed in
extent of item

Filmstrips
catalogued as a
set

DC   Newton, Stella Mary.
203   Napoleon [filmstrip] / compiled and annotated by Stella Mary
N49   Newton. -- London ; Toronto : Visual Publications, c1971.
1971   2 filmstrips : col. ; 35 mm. + 2 manuals ([32] p. ; 27 cm.).
-- (A Closer look into history ; 6-7)

        Contents: 1. The man and his surroundings (40 fr.) -- 2. His
effect on his time (37 fr.)
        Publisher's no.: CLH 6-7.

        1. Napoleon I, Emperor of the French.   I. Series.

Sample card 18[27]
3rd level

Secondary
position city in
the country of the
cataloguing
agency named

Accompanying
material listed in
full in physical
description area

Number of
frames listed in
contents note

Filmstrip set

693.21 Laying bricks to a line [filmstrip]. -- Chicago: Encyclopaedia
L453   Britannica Educational Corp., 1978.
     1 filmstrip cartridge (119 fr.) : sd., col. ; 16 mm. -- (Brick
masonry series)

     Duration: 76 min.
     For LaBelle projector.
     Programmed stops allow unrestricted response time.

     1. Bricklaying. I. Series.

Sound filmstrip
cartridge

641.3 Food [filmstrip]. -- Chicago : Encyclopaedia Britannica Educational
F739   Corp. ; Toronto : Visual Education Centre, c1973.
     12 filmslips ([13] fr. each) : col. ; 35 mm. + 12 sheets.

     Teachers' instructions printed on container.
     Intended audience: Beginning level of reading skill.

     1. Food.

Secondary
position publisher
in the country of
the cataloguing
agency named

Audience level

Accompanying
materials listed
briefly

Filmslip set

Flash Cards

Flash card: a card printed with words, numerals, or pictures, designed for rapid identification.

Flash cards may be organized in a picture file (see pages 103 to 105). Items of permanent value to the collection should be completely catalogued for their effective use.

The general rules on pages 17 to 22 apply with the following additions and exceptions.

Sources of information
The container is preferred to the accompanying data.

Physical description area
Extent of item. List the number of flash cards.

Option. If the general material designation "flash card" is used, the word "card(s)" may be substituted for "flash card(s)" (see sample card 21).

Other physical details. List sound only if it is integral.[28]
List b&w or col.

Dimensions. Height × width are listed in centimetres.

Care, handling, and storage
See General Guidelines for the Care, Handling, and Storage of Two-Dimensional, Opaque Materials on page 118.

513	Neureiter, Paul R.
Neu	Multiplication [flash card]. -- F.A. Owen, c1966.
	96 cards.

1. Arithmetic.   I. Title.

Sample card 21
1st level

Compare with
NBM/1 s.c. 55

QL Ebeling, Alfred W.
617   Teach-me about fishes flash cards [flash card] / Alfred W.
.2   Ebeling. -- Mineola, N.Y. : Renwal, c1968.
E24   48 flash cards : col. ; 7 × 5 cm. + 1 descriptive sheet
(3 p. ; 15 cm.). -- (Nature study cards) (Teach me)

Title on side of box: Fish flash cards.
Reproduction of original paintings by James Mason.
Text on verso.
Can also be used as study prints.

1. Fishes - North America.   I. Title.   II. Title: Fish flash
cards.

Sample card 22[29]
3rd level

More than one
series statement

513.2 Graded difficulty arithmetic program. Set I [flash card]. --
G754   [Chicago] : Bell & Howell, c1969.
200 flash cards : sd., b&w ; 9 × 23 cm. -- (Language Master
audio/visual instructional system card program)

For Language Master instructional device.
Intended audience: Primary grades.
Summary: Addition and subtraction facts to 20.

1. Arithmetic.   I. Series.

Sample card 23
2nd level

Sound flash card

Games

Game: a set of materials designed for play according to prescribed rules.

The general rules on pages 17 to 22 apply with the following additions and exceptions.

Physical description area

Extent of item. List the number of games in the item and add, if appropriate, in parentheses, the number and names of the pieces. When the number and/or type of pieces cannot be ascertained easily, the term "various pieces" is used.

Option. If the general material designation "game" is used, the term "1 game" may be omitted (see sample cards 24, 26).

Other physical details. List the material from which the item was made and col. or b&w, if such information is useful.

Dimensions. List the type of packaging and its dimensions in centimetres.

Note area

Notes may be essential to indicate use.

Care, handling, and storage

See General Guidelines for the Storage of Three-Dimensional Materials on page 118.

Sample card 24
1st level

Compare with
NBM/1 s.c. 56

```
793.7      Allen, Layman E.
ALL            Equations [game] : the game of creative mathematics. -- Science
           Research Associates, c1966.
               32 dice, 1 game board printed on container, 1 player's manual.




               1. Mathematical recreations.    I. Title.
```

Sample card 25
1st level

Quoted note

```
940.53     Smith, Daniel Caleb.
Smi            Trade-off at Yalta [game]. -- Scott Graphics, c1972.
               1 game (various pieces, 1 teacher's guide)

               "Offers ... firsthand experience in facing the problems that
           grew out of World War II"--Guide.




               1. Crimea Conference (1945 : Yalta).   I. Title.
```

793.74   Mathemax [game]. -- Kurralta Park, S. Aust. : Mathemax Pty.,
M42   1971.
           56 cards : col. ; in container, 7 × 10 × 3 cm. + 1 rule
sheet.

           Summary: Several mathematical games can be played with card
deck.

           1. Mathematical recreations.

LB   Richardson, Hazel A.
3031   Games for elementary school grades [game] / by Hazel A.
R52   Richardson. -- Minneapolis : Burgess, c1951.
1951   137 games on 154 cards : b&w ; in container, 12 × 17 × 4
cm.

           Subtitle on container: playground, gymnasium, classroom.
           Intended audience: Teachers.
           Summary: Basic principles for selection, preparation,
presentation, organization, and supervision of games for grades 1
to 6.

           (Continued on next card)

LB   Richardson, Hazel A. -- Games for elementary school grades
3031   [game] ... c1951.   (Card 2)
R52
1951   Includes index.
           ISBN 0-8087-1805-3.

           1. Games.   I. Title.

Globes

Globe: a sphere representing the earth, other celestial bodies, or the universe.

The general rules on pages 17 to 22 apply with the following additions and exceptions.

Sources of Information
Information for the catalogue record is taken from the following sources in this order:[31]

1. The item itself (Chief source of information);
2. Cradle and stand (Chief source of information);
3. Container (Chief source of information);
4. Accompanying material;
5. Other sources.

Mathematical data area

Scale. See **Maps** pages 48 to 53.

Physical description area
Extent of item. List the number of globes, celestial globes, or relief globes.[32]

Other physical details. List col. or b&w, the material from which the globe was made, if significant, and the mounting.

Dimensions. List the diameter in centimetres followed by the phrase "in diam."

Option. List the type of container followed by its dimensions (height × width × depth) in centimetres.

Care, handling, and storage
See General Guidelines for the Storage of Three-Dimensional Media on page 118.

---

912 [World globe] [globe]. -- Scale 1:41,849,600. -- Replogle, [1969?]
WOR 1 relief globe. -- (World nation series)
 	
     Title supplied by cataloguer.
     Manual for series by M. Guyette.
 	
     1. Earth.   2. Globes.
	Sample card 28
	1st level
	
	Compare with
	NBM/1 s.c. 60
	
	Note for series
	manual
	
	Relief globe

912   Geosphere globe [globe]. -- Scale 1:31,680,000. -- Chicago : Rand
G298   McNally, c1967.
         1 globe : col., mounted on metal stand ; 41 cm. in diam. + 1
manual. -- (Randmark ; IV/V)

         Shows political and physical data.
         Title from manual.
         Cradle base has directions, hours, attached hemisphere ring, and
half-circle arc.

         1. Earth.   2. Globes.

Sample card 29
2nd level

Globe with
accompanying
material

G   [Bathymetric globe] [globe]. -- Scale 1:41,817,600. 1 in. to 660
3171   miles. 1 cm. to 420 km. -- Chicago : Nystrom, [197-?]
C7   1 relief globe : col., plastic, mounted on plastic stand ; 31 cm.
B38   in diam. + 1 sound cassette (55 min. : $3^3/_4$ ips, mono.). -- (Man
and the ocean)

         Free ball globe in transparent plastic cradle on which cardinal
points of compass are given.
         Title on cassette: Using the bathymetric globe.

                (Continued on next card)

Sample card 30[33]
3rd level

Relief globe with
accompanying
material

G   [Bathymetric globe] [globe] ... [197-?]   (Card 2)
3171
C7   Title on container: Nystrom raised relief globe.
B38   Signals on cassette indicate appropriate pauses for classroom
discussion.
         Publisher's no.: OC-12 (on globe), OC-133 (on cassette)

         1. Ocean bottom.   I. Series.

Sample card 30
continued

Kits[34]

Kit: a set of material composed of many textual parts, or, two or more media, no one of which is identifiable as the predominant constituent of the item.

The general material designation "kit" is applied only to those media which are to be catalogued as a unit.

If one part of the item is clearly dominant, the item is not catalogued as a kit, but rather as the dominant medium, with the other media listed as accompanying material (see page 21 and sample cards 30, 48, 57, 91, etc.).

A media centre, which acquires a "kit" composed of two or more media packaged together, may choose to dismantle the set, discard the container, and catalogue each medium under its appropriate designation.

The general rules on pages 17 to 22 apply with the following additions and exceptions.

Sources of information
Information for the catalogue record is taken from the following sources in this order:

1. The container (Chief source of information);
2. The part which gives the most information (Chief source of information);
3. Other sources.

Main entry
A kit is entered under author where the author has been responsible for the creation of the kit as a whole. If each component has a different author, or if authorship of the kit as a whole cannot be established, enter under title.

Physical description area
If a full description of each part is not wanted, list the number and name of each type of material in the order of their importance[35] to the item as a whole. If this cannot be determined, list the number and name of each type of material in alphabetical order.[36] Follow this with the term "in container" and the container dimensions when appropriate.

If a full description of each part is wanted, list a description for each type of material on separate lines.

If the parts are difficult to name or their number makes precise identification impractical, such phrases as "18 various pieces" or "various pieces" may be used.

Care, handling, and storage
See General Guidelines for the Storage of Three-Dimensional Media on Page 118.

The sample cards for kits demonstrate some of the common cataloguing principles which should be applied to all nonbook materials. These principles are noted to the right of the card.

510   Mathlab [kit] / authors, J.W. Opper ... [et al.]. -- Scholar's
Mat   Choice, c1976.
          310 activity cards, 21 teacher's guide cards, 1 title card.

          Contents: Introduction -- Fractions and decimals -- Geometry --
Number fun -- Graphing -- Measurement.

        1. Mathematics.   I. Opper, J.W.

Parts listed in
order of
importance

389   Primary measurement with the Track 10 Bunch [kit]. -- Metric
PRI   Media, c1975.
          1 die, 1 marker, 6 posters, 1 rope, 1 song sheet, 7
transparency masters.

        1. Metric system.   2. Measurement.

Parts listed
alphabetically

372.4   The Farling finds out about toys [kit] / author, the Education
Far   Workshop, Inc. -- General Learning Corp., c1970.
          1 filmslip, 1 sound disc.

          Filmslip mounted in rigid format for use with : Phono-viewer.
Script on inside cover of container.

        1. Language arts.   2. Toys.   I. Education Workshop.

Special
equipment note
(see pages 21 to 22
for discussion)

549
R592
    Rocks and minerals kit [kit] / National Film Board of Canada for
the Department of Mines and Technical Surveys = Initiation
aux minéraux / l'Office national du film, Canada pour le
compte du Ministère des mines et des relevés techniques. --
[Montreal] : N.F.B.C., [1964?]
    1 chart, 3 filmstrips, 1 manual, 1 map, 5 pamphlets, 13 rocks
and minerals ; in container, 34 × 28 × 5 cm.

    One pamphlet only in French and English.

                       (Continued on next card)

Sample card 34[37]
2nd level

Compare with
NBM/1 s.c. 63

549
R592
    Rocks and minerals kit [kit] ... [1964?]   (Card 2)

    1. Mines and mineral resources - Canada.   2. Mineralogy -
Canada.   3. Rocks.   I. Canada. Dept. of Energy, Mines and
Resources.

Sample card 34
(continued)

510
Un2
    Understanding numbers for beginners [kit]. -- Springfield, Mass. :
Milton Bradley, c1963.
    52 cards, 2 instruction cards ; in container, 11 × 18 × 4 cm.

    Title from container.
    Can be used as flash cards and for playing 3 games.

    1. Number concept.   2. Mathematical recreations.

Sample card 35
2nd level

Item which can
be used as more
than one material
(see page 18)

Sample card 36
2nd level

372. Reading and spelling with phonics [kit]. -- Arlington Heights,
4145 Ill. : Reading Development Center, c1964.
R227 8 charts, 1 instruction booklet, 4 sound discs ; in container,
23 × 36 × 3 cm.

  Editor, Margaret Deats.

Editor not named
in chief sources
of information

  1. Reading (Elementary) - Phonetic method. I. Reading
Development Center.

Sample card 37
2nd level

709. Evans, Grose.
034 19th century developments in art [kit] / author-consultant-narrator,
Ev15 Grose Evans. -- [Chicago] : Society for Visual Education, c1969.
  40 slides, 1 sound disc ; in container, 32 × 33 × 8 cm.

Compare with
NBM/1 s.c. 109

  1. Art, Modern - 19th century - History. I. Title.

Sample card 38
3rd level

RT Nursing [kit] : the challenge of caring / International Cinemedia
82 Center for the Directors of Nursing Committee, Montreal Joint
N87 Hospital Institute. -- Canada : I.C.C., c1976.
1976 1 filmstrip (80 fr.) : col. ; 35 mm.
  1 pamphlet ([2] p.) ; 22 cm.
  1 sound cassette (ca. 7 min.) : 3³⁄₄ ips, mono.

  Direction, Ian Ferguson ; photography, John Sleeman ; script,
Michael McCormick Jr. ; production, Martin Rosenbaum. --
Cassette pulsed for manual and automatic projectors. --

Subtitle

Place unknown,
country listed[38]

Physical
description on
separate lines

Notes in one
paragraph

(Continued on next card)

Sample card 38
(continued)

RT
82
N87
1976

Nursing [kit] ... c1976.   (Card 2)

Intended audience: Those considering a career in nursing; pamphlet
only for Quebec province residents. -- Producer's number: 0321,
0322.

1. Nursing as a profession.   I. Montreal Joint Hospital
Institute. Directors of Nursing Committee.

Sample card 39[39]
3rd level

GB
612
W39

Way, Ruth.
    Hot deserts [kit] / Ruth Way. -- London ; Toronto : Visual
Publications, [1975?]
        1 filmstrip (39 fr.) : col. ; 35 min.
        1 sound cassette (ca. 18 min.) : 3³/₄ ips, mono.
        4 study prints : col. ; 29 × 88 cm. folded to 29 × 44 cm.
        1 manual (15 p.) ; 22 cm.
        1 question sheet ([4] p.) ; 22 cm. --
(The Earth & man. The Earth without man ; 4)

Physical
description given
on separate lines

(Continued on next card)

Sample card 39
(continued)

GB
612
W39

Way, Ruth. -- Hot deserts [kit] ... [1975?]   (Card 2)

Pictures on filmstrip and study prints identical.
Cassette has automatic and advance signals.

1. Deserts.   I. Title.   II. Series.

Machine-Readable Data Files

Machine-readable data file: information coded by methods that require the use of a machine (typically, but not always a computer) for processing. Examples include files stored on magnetic tape, punched cards, aperture cards, disk packs, etc.

The general rules on pages 17 to 22 apply with the following additions and exceptions.

Sources of information
Information for the catalogue record is taken from the following sources in this order:

1. The internal user label (Chief source of information);
2. Documentation issued by the file creator (Chief source of information if there is no internal user label);
3. Other published descriptions of the file;
4. Other sources, including the file container, labels, etc.

Title and statement of responsibility area
A data set name is not normally considered to be a title proper.

File description area
Extent of item. Enumerate the major type of file using one of the following terms: data file (the file containing the information), program file (the file containing the instructions to the machine), or object program (the computer language program). Some machine-readable data files contain all three types: data, program, and object. Whichever is the major is listed in the extent of the item, and the other(s) are included as accompanying material.

Add in parentheses the number of logical records for a data file, or the number of statements and the name of the programming language for a program file, or the name, number, etc., of the machine on which an object program runs.

Accompanying material. List files not given in the extent of item as accompanying material, optionally including additional information in parentheses, e.g., 1 data file (2,500 logical records) + 1 program file, or 1 data file (2,500 logical records) + 1 program file (300 statements, COBOL).

List codebooks, manuals, etc. as accompanying material. A variety of accompanying materials of minor individual significance may be listed using the term "associated documents."

Note area
List the program version and/or level.

List the ISBN of codebooks.

List any restrictions on the general availability of the file such as date restrictions, restrictions on types of users, etc.

List the equipment required if the file cannot be used on the facilities available to the media centre.

Care, handling, and storage
Care, handling, and storage of machine-readable data is dependent upon the format of the file. The data itself can be mechanically transferred from one format to another, e.g., punched card to tape. Media centres in the future will undoubtedly acquire material in one format and transfer it to any format required.

Access to machine-readable data files may also come from on-line access to files stored in major centres through the cathode ray tube present in the media centre. In such cases, the care, handling, and storage of the files is not germane to the media centre.

Some of the formats are discussed on pages 115 to 119. Specialized publications should be consulted for detailed treatment of this subject.

<table>
<tr><td>

882
AES

Aeschylus.
    [Selections. Machine-readable data file]
    [Plays] / prepared by Henrik Holmboe. -- Institute for
Linguistics Aarhus Universitet ; American Philological Association,
[distributor], 1978.
    5 data files + 1 codebook.

    In Greek.
    Title supplied by cataloguer.
    Prepared from: Aeschyli septem quae supersunt tragoediae /
recensuit Gilbertus Murray. Ed. 2. Oxonii : E Typograheo
Clarendoniano, 1955.

                  (Continued on next card)

</td></tr>
</table>

Sample card 40
1st level

Uniform title

<table>
<tr><td>

882
AES

Aeschylus. -- [Selections. Machine-readable data file] ... 1978.
    (Card 2)

    Size of file unknown.
    Contents: Agamemnon -- Persae -- Prometheus vinctus --
Septum contra Thelsae -- Supplices.

    I. Holmboe, Henrik.   II. Murray, Gilbert, ed.

</td></tr>
</table>

Sample card 40
(continued)

Designation of
function in added
entry

<table>
<tr><td>

324.2
0994
Ai93

Aitken, Donald.
    Australian national political attitudes [machine-readable data file]
/ principal investigators, Donald Aitken, Michael Kahan, Donald
E. Stokes. -- Canberra : Australian National University, Australian
Survey Project, 1976.
    2 data files (16,860,430 logical records) + 1 codebook.

    Summary: A post-election study focused on the national election
of October 25, 1969. Includes demographic data.

    1. Australia. Parliament. House of Representatives - Elections.
I. Kahan, Michael.   II. Stokes, Donald E.   III. Title.

</td></tr>
</table>

Sample card 41
2nd level

Sample card 42
3rd level

Z   Hershey, Allen V.
253.3   A contribution to computer typesetting techniques
H47   [machine-readable data file] / principal investigator, Allen V.
        Hershey. -- Washington : U.S. Dept. of Commerce, National
        Bureau of Standards, Office of Standard Reference Data ;
        Springfield, Va. : U.S. Dept. of Commerce, National Technical
        Information Service, 1978.
            2 data files (4,034, 3,760 logical records) + 1 codebook (25
        p. ; 23 cm.)

            Title from: NTIS computer products catalog data sheet.

                        (Continued on next card)

Sample card 42
(continued)

Z   Hershey, Allan V. -- A contribution to computer typesetting
253.3   techniques [machine-readable data file] ... 1978.   (Card 2)
H47
            Alternate title: Hershey's tables.
            Contents: Occidental type fonts and graphic symbols -- Katakan,
        Hiragana, and Kanji characters.
            Date of study: 1967-1972.
            PB 263 925.

            1. Computerized typesetting - Tables.   2. Computer output
        microform devices.   I. Title.

Maps

Map: a flat representation of part or all of either the earth or the universe.

Maps and relief models are included under this heading and designated by the term "map."

Maps may be organized as ephemeral materials (see pages 103 to 105). Items of permanent value to the collection should be completely catalogued for their effective use.

The general rules on pages 17 to 22 apply with the following additions and exceptions.

Sources of information
Information for the catalogue record is taken from the following sources in this order:[40]

1. The item itself (Chief source of information). If two or more titles are given on the face of the map, preference is given in the following order:
   a) The most appropriate title,
   b) The title within the border of the map,
   c) The title in the margin;
2. Container or case (Chief source of information);
3. Accompanying material;
4. Other sources.

Title and statement of responsibility area
If the title information does not indicate a geographic area, supply as other title information a word or phrase in square brackets stating the region covered in the map.

Mathematical data area
Scale. List the term "Scale" and a representative fraction expressed as a ratio, e.g., Scale 1:1,000,000. Natural scale indicators for conversion of graphic scales to representative fractions are commercially available, or the mathematically inclined can use the following method. If scale is given in terms of miles to an inch, multiply the number of miles per inch (1 in. = 43 mi.) by the number of inches in a mile (63,360 in.) For example, $43 \times 63,360 = 2,724,480$ is listed as Scale 1:2,724,480.

If a scale is taken from an outside source, it is enclosed in square brackets.

If no scale is found, use a bar graph, grid, or comparison with the scale of a similar map to determine one. Such a representative fraction is preceded by the term "ca."

The terms "Scale indeterminable," "Scale varies," "Scales vary," and "Not drawn to scale" are listed when appropriate.

Option. List additional scale information found on the item (see sample card 46).

In three-dimensional items, such as relief models, the vertical scale is also listed if known.

Scale is always listed in the first level of description.

Projection. List projection if it is found in the first three sources of information.

Option. List meridians, parallels, and/or ellipsoid.

Statement of coordinates and equinox. This is optional. See the *Anglo-American Cataloguing Rules*, 2nd edition, rule 3.3D for details of this rule.

Punctuation. Representative fraction scale information is separated from other scale information by a period-space (.), and scale as a whole from projection by a space-semicolon-space (;). Coordinates and equinox are enclosed in parentheses and separated from each other by a space-semicolon-space (;).

Physical description area
Extent of item. List the number of aerial charts, aerial remote sensing images, anamorphic maps, bird's eye views or map views, block diagrams, celestial charts, charts, hydrographic charts, imaginative maps, maps, map profiles, map sections, orthophotos, photo mosaics (controlled), photo mosaics (uncontrolled), photomaps, plans, relief models, remote sensing images, space remote sensing images, terrestrial remote sensing images, topographic drawings, topographic prints.

If there is more than 1 map on a sheet or if several sheets comprise one map, state this concisely, e.g., 3 aerial charts on 1 sheet, 1 map in 3 sections.

Other physical details. List col. or b&w, the material from which the map was made, if significant, and the mounting, if appropriate.

Dimensions. Height × width of the face of the map between the neat lines are listed in centimetres. If the map is circular, list the diameter in centimetres followed by the phrase "in diam." For irregularly shaped maps list the greatest dimensions or, if these are difficult to determine, the dimensions of the sheet itself; e.g., on sheet 60 × 78 cm.

Option. Add depth to measurements for relief models.

Those wishing to describe precisely the dimensions of maps in sections, folded maps, maps of different sizes, etc. should consult the *Anglo-American Cataloguing Rules*, 2nd edition, rule 3.5D1.

Note area

List mathematical and other cartographic data that is considered useful to the media centre's patrons.

List insets.

910.1
CRA
Cram's geographical terms [map]. -- Not drawn to scale. -- G.F. Cram, [19--]
2 imaginative maps on 1 sheet.

Terminology described pictorially.

1. Geography - Terminology.

912
W893
The World [map] / prepared from reproductive material provided by the Surveys and Mapping Branch, Department of Energy, Mines and Resources of Canada. -- Scale 1:35,000,000 ; Van der Grinten proj. -- New Westminster, B.C. : Open Trails, [19--]
1 map : col., plastic ; 73 × 114 cm.

Includes Canadian air distances in statute miles and distance between Canadian ports in nautical miles. -- Insets: Arctic ; Antarctica ; The southern sky ; The northern sky.

1. World maps.   I. Canada. Surveys and Mapping Branch.

936.   Ordnance Survey map of Roman Britain [map]. -- 3rd ed.,
204   Reprinted with minor corrections. -- Scale 1:1,000,000 ; Conical
Or2   proj. -- Chessington, Surrey : Ordnance Survey, 1956.
            1 map : col. ; 97 × 75 cm.

            Shows all known Roman sites.
            Inset: Shetland and Orkney Islands.

            1. Gt. Brit. - History - Roman period, 55 B.C.-449 A.D.
        I. Gt. Brit. Ordnance Survey.   II. Title: Roman Britain.

Sample card 45
2nd level

Compare with
NBM/1 s.c. 69

Subsequent
edition statement

Map

---

930   Knowlton, Daniel C.
K765   Migrations of the peoples in the fifth century [map] / Daniel
        C. Knowlton, T. Walter Wallbank. -- Scale 1:4,752,000. 1 in. to
        75 miles. -- Chicago : Nystrom, [19--]
            1 map : col. ; 84 × 116 cm. folded to 25 × 32 cm. --
        (Knowlton-Wallbank world history maps ; 7)

            Title on wrapper: Migrations in the fifth century.
            Series on wrapper: World history.

                                    (Continued on next card)

Sample card 46
2nd level

Additional scale
information

Projection not
given on item

Variant title and
series title

Folded map

---

930   Knowlton, Daniel C. -- Migrations of the peoples in the fifth
K765   century [map] ... [19--]   (Card 2)

            Inset: Germanic settlements within the Roman Empire about 450
        A.D. Scale 1:14,256,000.

            1. Rome - History - 392-814.   2. Migrations of nations.
        I. Wallbank, T. Walter.   II. Title.

Sample card 46
(continued)

G
3401
C9
C35
1975

Canada [map] : isoclinic chart 1975.0 / Division of
Geomagnetism, Earth Physics Branch, Dept. of Energy, Mines
and Resources = Canada : carte isocline 1975.0 / Division du
géomagnétisme, Direction de la physique du globe, Ministère de
l'énergie, des mines et des ressources. -- Scale 1:10,000,000 ;
Lambert conformal conical proj., standard parallels 49° and 77°,
modified polyconic proj. north of latitude 80°. -- Ottawa : The
Dept., [1975?]
1 chart : col. ; 54 × 58 cm.

Shows magnetic repeat stations and magnetic observatories.

(Continued on next card)

Parallel titles and
statements of
responsibility

Associated
projection
information

Chart

G
3401
C9
C35
1975

Canada [map] isoclinic chart 1975.0 ... [1975?]   (Card 2)

Publisher's no: 1.1975.0.

1. Magnetism, Terrestrial - Canada.   I. Canada. Earth Physics
Branch.   II. Title: Canada [map] : carte isocline 1975.0.

523.3
Ea76

The Earth's moon [map]. -- Scale ca. 1:7,200,000 ; orthographic
proj. -- Chicago : Nystrom, c1969.
2 maps on 1 sheet (1 attached overlay) : col. ; 77 cm. in
diam. each on sheet 162 × 121 cm. -- (Man in space)

Shows near and far sides of moon.
Near side adapted from the World book atlas map based on
U.S. Air Force photographic mosaic; far side adapted from
original art based on U.S.A.F. lunar chart.

(Continued on next card)

Map with
accompanying
material

Sample card 48
(continued)

523.3   The Earth's moon [map] ... c1969.   (Card 2)
Ea76
         Accompanied by 1 sound tape cassette titled: Using the moon
    map (ca. 30 min.)

Accompanying
material listed in
notes

         1. Moon.   I. Title: Using the moon map.   II. Series.

○

Sample card 49
3rd level

G   Hose, Ian.
3401   Geography of Canada [map] / designed by Ian Hose. -- Not
E6   drawn to scale. -- Downsview, Ont. : McIntyre, [197-?]
H68   2 maps : col., flannel ; 60 × 88 cm. in plastic case,
1970z   31 × 40 cm. + 1 manual (8 p. ; 22 cm.)

         Two flannelgraphs with ca. 100 flannel overlays.
         Contents: Physical background -- Political background.

         1. Canada - Maps.   I. Title.

Flannel board
map

○

Sample card 50
1st level

551.4   Chase, Thomas E.
CHA   Ocean features model [map]. -- Scale indeterminable. -- T.N.
         Hubbard, [19--]
             1 relief model + 1 lesson plan.

             "Relief exaggerated"--Lesson plan.

Quoted note

         1. Ocean.   I. Title.

Relief model with
accompanying
material

○

```
G         Nystrom raised relief model of geographical terms [map]. -- Not
108           drawn to scale. -- Chicago : Nystrom, c1958.
M6        1 relief model : col., plastic ; 96 × 107 × 2 cm.
N98
          Glossary outside border of map (77 × 107 cm.) and selected
        terms on verso of class set of maps.
          Includes class set of desk maps and manual (36 p.) titled:
        Teaching geographical terms with the Nystrom relief model / by
        Frank D. Huttlinger.

          1. Geography - Terminology.
```

Relief model with
2 accompanying
materials listed in
note area

Topographic series of maps

A topographic series is a group of sheets, depicting general physical and cultural details, in which contiguous areas are mapped in the same scale and in accordance with a uniform set of symbols and mapping standards. The relation of one sheet to another is usually indicated by a small scale index map.

Topographic sheets in a series need not be listed individually in the catalogue. Only the top or index sheet may be listed. The index sheet is consulted to find the individual sheets in the series.

The index sheet may be fully catalogued. An easier and adequate method of catalogue listing is by reference entry, as shown below.

```
Canada. Topographic series. 1:250,000.

To find maps held in this series, see map drawer 6, index
sheet no. 18.
```

The individual maps in the series held by the media centre and their respective locations are indicated on the index sheet.

Care, handling, and storage

See General Guidelines for the Care, Handling, and Storage of Two-Dimensional, Opaque Materials on page 118.

Microforms

Microform: a miniature reproduction of printed or other graphic matter which cannot be utilized without magnification.

Microfilms, microfiches, microopaques, and aperture cards are included under this heading and designated by the term "microform."

The general rules on pages 17 to 22 apply with the following additions and exceptions.

Sources of information
Information for the catalogue record is taken from the following sources in this order:

1. The item itself (Chief source of information). In *microfilms* preference is given to the information on the title frame(s). If the information from this source is inadequate or nonexistent, data is drawn from the rest of the item including a container which is an integral part of the item.

    In *microfiches* and *microopaques* preference is given to information on the title frame(s), secondarily to the eye-readable data on the top of the item, and thirdly from the rest of the item.

    In *aperture cards* preference is given to information on the title card(s).
2. Container;
3. Accompanying eye-readable material;
4. Other sources.

Material specific details area
Do not use this area unless:

1. A cartographic item has been reproduced in microform.[42] In this case, follow the rules under Mathematical data area on page 48.

2. A serial has been reproduced in microform. In this case, list numeric and/or chronological data, such as volume or issue number(s), date(s) of issue. (See sample card 60.)

Physical description area
Extent of item. List the number of aperture cards, microfiches, microfilms or microopaques. If appropriate, add the terms "cartridge," "cassette," or "reel."

> *Option*. If a general material designation is used, the prefix "micro" may be omitted from the specific material designation (see sample cards 53, 59, 61).

Microfiches. List the number of frames in parentheses,[43] if this can be ascertained easily.

Other physical details. If appropriate, list negative; positive is not recorded.

List col.; b&w is not given, this being the norm for microforms.

List illustrations; the manner of listing illustrations is similar to that for books.

Dimensions.
Aperture cards, microfiches, microopaques. Height × width are listed in centimetres.
Microfilms. If the reel is other than 3 inches in diameter, list this fact in inches (see sample card 60).
List the width of the film in millimetres.

Note area
Reduction ratio. Most microform readers in common use in media centres can accommodate materials with a 16−30× reduction. A reduction ratio outside this range should be noted using the following terms:

Low reduction — up to an inclusive of 15×
High reduction — 31× to 60×
Very high reduction — 61× to 90×
Ultra high reduction — above 90×. In this range the specific ratio is also given (see sample card 56)
Reduction ratio varies

Some microforms, particularly COM catalogues and union lists, require a particular lens in a multi-lens reader or a particular reader. In these cases the exact reduction ratio is needed for machine selection, e.g., Reduction ratio, 24×.

Reader. The name of the intended reader for cassette or cartridge containers is noted, because containers are not interchangeable in every reader (see sample card 59).

Option. List type of film used, e.g., Silver based film.

Original format. If the microform was published originally in another format, the bibliographic details of this publication are noted.

Care, handling, and storage
See General Guidelines for the Care, Handling, and Storage of Film Media on page 116.

Sample card 53
1st level

568	Blough, Glenn O.
BLO	Discovering dinosaurs [microform]. -- Xerox, [197-]
	1 fiche (42 fr.)

Microreproduction of original published: McGraw-Hill, 1960.

1. Dinosaurs.   I. Title.

Microfiche

Sample card 54
2nd level

025.46	Croghan, Antony.
C875	A thesaurus-classification for the physical forms of non-book media [microform] / by Antony Croghan. -- 2nd ed. -- London : Coburgh Publications, 1976.
	1 microfiche (53 fr.) : negative ; 11 × 15 cm.

Edition area

Title on fiche heading: A thesaurus-classification for forms of non-book media.
First ed. published 1970 in book format.
Date on fiche heading: 1977.

1. Audio-visual materials.   I. Title.

Microfiche

150	James, William, 1842-1920.
J237	The principles of psychology [microform] / W. James. -- [Chicago] : Library Resources, c1970.
	2 microfiches : ill. ; 8 × 13 cm.
	Very high reduction.
	Microreproduction of original published: London : Macmillan, 1891. 2v. : ill. ; 23 cm.
	1. Psychology. I. Title.

○

Sample card 55
2nd level

Author's dates added

Number of frames not easily ascertained

Reduction ratio

Compare with NBM/1 s.c. 79

Microfiche

E	Craven, John.
467.1	Prison life of Jefferson Davis [microform] / John Craven. --
D26	[S.l.] : National Cash Register, [196-?]
C9	1 microfiche ; 11 × 15 cm. -- (PCMI collection)
	Ultra high reduction, 150 ×.
	With: General Sherman / M. Force -- Life and campaigns of Major-General J.E.B. Stuart / H. McClennen -- General Butler in New Orleans / J. Parton -- Life and public services of Ambrose

(Continued on next card)

○

Sample card 56
3rd level

Item without a collective title

Compare with NBM/1 s.c. 80

Reduction ratio

"With note"

Microfiche

E	Craven, John. -- Prison life of Jefferson Davis [microform] ...
467.1	[196-?] (Card 2)
D26	
C9	E. Burnside / B. Poore -- Life of General George G. Meade / R. Bache.
	Microreproduction of original published: New York : Carleton, c1966. 377 p. ; 19 cm.
	1. Davis, Jefferson, I. Title.

○

Sample card 56
(continued)

686.43   Introduction to micrographics [microform] / prepared by National
In8   Microfilm Association. -- Silver Spring, Md. : The Association,
            c1974.
            2 microfiches (66 fr.) : all ill., col. ; 11 × 15 cm. + 1 sound
        cassette + 1 reading script. -- (Personal learning package ; PLP1)

        Sound cassette has audible signals.

        1. Microforms.   I. National Micrographics Association.

Microfiches with
2 accompanying
materials

E   Robert Woods Bliss Collection of Pre-Columbian Art.
59   Pre-Columbian art [microform] / edited by Elizabeth P. Benson.
A7   -- Chicago : University of Chicago Press, c1976.
H34   1 microfiche (82 fr.) : all ill., col. ; 11 × 15 cm. + 1
1976   manual (16 p. : ill. ; 21 cm.). -- (A University of Chicago Press
        text/fiche)

        At head of title: Dumbarton Oaks collections.
        ISBN 0-226-68981-6.

                                 (Continued on next card)

Entry under
corporate body

Microfiche with
accompanying
material

E   Robert Woods Bliss Collection of Pre-Columbian Art. --
59   Pre-Columbian art [microform] ... c1976.   (Card 2)
A7
H34
1976

        1. Indians - Art - Catalogs.   2. Bliss, Robert Woods - Art
collections.   3. Indians - Antiquities - Catalogs.   4. America -
Antiquities - Catalogs.   I. Benson, Elizabeth P.   II. Title.   III.
Title: Dumbarton Oaks collections.

```
027        Donnelly, Francis Dolores.
.571           The National Library of Canada [microform]. -- University
DON        Microfilms, 1974.
               1 film cartridge.

               For Information Design reader.
               Microreproduction of original: Thesis (Ph.D) -- University of
           Illinois at Urbana-Champaign, 1971.


               1. National Library of Canada - History.

                        ◯
```

Sample card 59
1st level

Microfilm
cartridge

```
020.5      American libraries [microform] / American Library Association. --
Am35           Vol. 1, no. 1 (Jan. 1970)-              . -- Ann Arbor,
           Mich. : University Microfilms, 1971-
               microfilm reels : ill. ; 4 in., 16 mm. -- (Current
           periodical series)

               Issued every month except bimonthly July-August.
               Continues: ALA bulletin.
               Includes index.
               Publication no.: 5731-S.
               ISSN 0002-9769.
                        ◯         (Continued on next card)
```

Sample card 60
3rd level

Open entry

Materials specific
details area

ISSN
Microfilm

```
020.5      American libraries [microform] ... 1971-          (Card 2)
Am35




               1. Library science - Periodicals.    I. American Library
           Association.    II. Title: ALA bulletin.
                        ◯
```

Sample card 60
(continued)

```
977        Early narratives of the Northwest [microform] / edited by Louise
EAR          Phelps Kellogg. -- Micro-card Corp., 1963.
             10 opaques on 5 cards.

             Microreproduction of original published: T.J. Brown, 1865.




             1. America - Exploration.   2. Northwest, Old - Exploring
           expeditions.   I. Kellogg, Louise Phelps.
```

Sample card 61[44]
1st level

Compare with
NBM/1 s.c. 78

Microopaque

```
676        [Hicks & Brown Paper Ltd.] first floor plan [microform]. --
.230223      [S.1.] : Microfilm Graphic Corp., [19--]
H529         1 aperture card : negative, all ill. ; 8 × 13 cm.

             Technical drawing.




             1. Paper mills - Design and construction.   2. Floor space,
           Industrial.
```

Sample card 62
2nd level

Part of title
supplied

Place and date
not known

Aperture card

Microscope Slides

Microscope slide: a specialized slide produced specifically for use with a microscope or micro-projector.

Microscope slides may be organized in slide trays (see pages 103 to 105). Items of permanent value to the collection should be completely catalogued for their effective use.

The general rules on pages 17 to 22 apply with the following additions and exceptions.

Physical description area
Extent of item. List the number of microscope slides.

Option. If the general material designation "microscope slide" is used, the term "slide(s)" may be substituted for "microscope slide(s)" (see sample card 63).

Other physical details. If the microscope slide is made of material other than glass, list this material.

If a microscope slide is stained, list this.

Dimensions. List length × width in centimetres. When an item is packaged, the type of package and its dimensions in centimetres are given.

Note area
Type of stain and the particular aspect of the slide the stain highlights is noted, if applicable.

Method of preparation, e.g., sectioning, orientation, material in which specimen is imbedded, spread, smear, whole mount, etc., is noted.

Care, handling, and storage
See General Guidelines for the Care, Handling, and Storage of Microscope Slides on page 117.

Sample card 63
1st level

Compare with
NBM/1 s.c. 83

632   Apple scab [microscope slide]. -- A. Reid Enterprises, [197-?]
APP   18 slides.

        Classroom set containing similar sections of the scab.

        1. Apples - Diseases and pests.

641.3   Foods [microscope slide]. -- Newark, N.J. : Aristo-Craft, c1960.
F739   6 microscope slides ; 2 × 5 cm. in case, 13 × 17 cm.

           Descriptive sheet mounted on case.
           Contents: Potato starch -- Bean starch -- Starch grain -- Bread
yeast -- Beer yeast -- Wine yeast.

           1. Starch.   2. Yeast.

Slide set

QH   Drosophila salivary gland chromosomes [microscope slide]. --
470   Burlington, N.C. : Carolina Biological Supply, [197-?]
D7   1 slide : stained ; 3 × 8 cm.
D76

           Smear.
           Aceto-orcein stain shows giant polytene chromosomes with
clearly visible banding.

           1. Drosophila.   2. Chromosomes.

Models

Model: a three-dimensional representation of an object, either exact or to scale; a mock-up.

The general rules on pages 17 to 22 apply with the following additions and exceptions.

Physical description area
Extent of item. List the number of models in the item and add, if appropriate, in parentheses the number of pieces. When the number of pieces cannot be ascertained easily, the term "various pieces" may be used.

Option. If the general material designation "model" is used, the term "1 model" may be omitted (see sample card 66).

Other physical details. List the material from which the item was made and the colour. If the item is in one or two colours, state these colours.

Dimensions. List the dimensions in centimetres with, if necessary, a word or phrase identifying the dimension. When an item is packaged, list the type of package and its dimensions.

Note area
Scale is listed if this information is useful.

Care, handling, and storage
See General Guidelines for the Storage of Three-Dimensional Media on Page 118.

Sample card 66
1st level

```
551.6      Weather model [model]. -- T.N. Hubbard, c1963.
WEA           5 pieces.




              1. Weather.
                              ◯
```

Sample card 67[45]
2nd level

611.71   Human skeleton model [model]. -- Oak Lawn, Ill. : Ideal School
H88   Supply, c1964.
           1 model (2 pieces) : plastic, white, hung from metal stand ; 30
cm. high. -- (Human anatomy group ; S228)

        Scale model.
        Notes by Jack Megenity.

        1. Bones.   2. Skeleton.   I. Series: Human anatomy group ;
S228 [model]

Compare with
NBM/1 s.c. 85

General material
designation
added to series
tracing. See page
12 for
explanation

Sample card 68
3rd level

QM   The Human brain kit [model]. -- Skokie, Ill. : Lindberg, c1974.
455   1 model (4 pieces) ; plastic ; in box, 36 × 26 × 6 cm. + 1
H84   guide (4 p. : ill. ; 28 cm.). -- (Natural science series ; kit no.
1974   1306)

        Title on container: The human brain : an anatomically accurate
plastic construction kit.
        Fits into Human skull kit, no. 1301.
        Life size model dissected into 4 sections.
        Designed to be permanently or impermanently coloured.

        1. Brain.   I. Series.

Variant title
noted

Motion Pictures

Motion picture: film, with or without sound, bearing a sequence of images which creates the illusion of movement when projected.

Loops, cartridges, cassettes, kinescopes, stock shots, trailers, etc., are included under this heading and designated by the term "motion picture."

The *Anglo-American Cataloguing Rules*, 2nd edition, chapter 7, should be consulted by those cataloguing stock shots, commercials, trailers, newsfilm, and unedited material.

The general rules on pages 17 to 22 apply with the following additions and exceptions.

Title and statement of responsibility area
Statements of responsibility. List those persons or bodies who are considered to be of major importance to the work or to the media centre's patrons. Other persons or bodies who have contributed to the work may be listed in the note area (see below under **Note area**).

Publication, distribution, etc. area
Name of publisher, distributor, etc. The publisher, distributor, releasing agent, etc., is listed. A producer or production agency which has not been named in the statement of responsibility is also given.

Physical description area
Extent of item. List the number of film cartridges, film cassettes, film loops, or film reels.

> *Option*. If a general material designation is used, the word "film" may be omitted from the specific material designation (see sample cards 69, 70, 73).

List in parentheses a trade name[46] if the use of the item is conditional upon this information (see sample cards 70, 78).

List in parentheses after the specific material designation the total playing time stated on the item, its packaging, or its accompanying material. If duration is not stated, an approximate time, e.g., (ca. 50 min.), is listed if it can be ascertained easily. If the item is in parts and the parts have the same or almost the same duration, phrases such as (15 min. each) or (ca. 15 min. each) may be used.

Other physical details. If appropriate, list the aspect ratio and special projection characteristics, for example, Cinerama, stereoscopic, etc. If this cannot be done succinctly, list the information in the note area.

List sd., si., or si. at sd. speed.

List b&w or col. Sepia is listed as "b&w."

List playing speed in frames per second, if this is useful information.

Dimensions. List width in millimetres. For 8 mm., preface the dimensions with one of the following: Maurer, single, standard, super.

Media centres, which have chosen 1st level description and which contain more than one motion picture format, must have enough information listed in the physical description area to enable the patron to identify necessary equipment. Whether a film is sound or silent and the gauge of the film are essential data for the selection of equipment (see sample card 69).

Note area
List featured performers or other participants not given elsewhere in the record. The names are prefaced by an appropriate term such as Cast, Presenter, Narrator, Credits and, if appropriate, a statement of function. Cast may be listed as part of a contents note.

List the date of original production if it differs from the date(s) listed in the publication, distribution, etc. area.

List other physical details which affect use, such as magnetic sound track, negative print, three-dimensional film, etc.

Summary. An objective and succinct summary of the content and intended use is necessary for many films. If appropriate, information on technique, cast, and audience level may be included.

Care, handling, and storage
See General Guidelines for the Care, Handling, and Storage of Film Media on page 116.

Sample card 69
1st level

813
MEE

Meet John Doe [motion picture] / directed by Frank Capra. --
[Abridged ed.]. -- Thunderbird Films, 1974.
1 reel (20 min.) : sd. ; super 8 mm.

Cast: Gary Cooper, Barbara Stanwyck, and others.
Shorter version of the 1941 motion picture of the same name.
Summary: An unemployed man, built into the symbol of ''the
average man'' by a newspaper, rebels when he realizes how he is
being used.

I. Cooper, Gary.   II. Stanwyck, Barbara.   III. Capra, Frank.

Edition statement

Super 8 sound

Sample card 70[47]
2nd level

915.1132
C441

China, cities in transition [motion picture]. -- [Santa Ana, Calif.] :
Doubleday Multimedia, 1969.
1 cartridge (Technicolor) (18 min.) : sd., col. ; super 8 mm. --
(Red China series)

Notes on container.
Summary: The growth and nature of Shanghai are shown with
contrasts between traditional and modern modes of life.

1. Shanghai - Description.   2. Housing - China.   I. Series.

Compare with
NBM/1 s.c. 88

Sound motion
picture loop

Sample card 71
2nd level

179.9
W574

Whether to tell the truth [motion picture] / edited by Visual
Consultants in association with the English Dept., Briarcliffe
High School. -- [New York] : Learning Corp. of America,
c1972.
1 film reel (14 min.) : sd., b&w ; 16 mm. + 1 study guide.
-- (Searching for values : a film anthology)

Cast: Marlon Brando, and others.
Edited from the 1954 motion picture entitled: On the
waterfront / directed by Elia Kazan.
Summary: Illegal activities on the docks present the conflict
between duty to friends and duty to society.

(Continued on next card)

Series subtitle

Relationship to
other work

<table>
<tr><td>

179.9
W574

Whether to tell the truth [motion picture] ... c1972.   (Card 2)

</td><td>

Sample card 71
(continued)

</td></tr>
</table>

179.9
W574

Whether to tell the truth [motion picture] ... c1972.   (Card 2)

1. Truthfulness and falsehood.   2. Ethics - Case studies.
I. On the waterfront [motion picture]   II. Brando, Marlon.
II. Kazan, Elia.   III. Series: Searching for values.

General material
designation used
in added entry.
See page 12 for
explanation

Sample card 72
2nd level

784
M973

Music sequence [motion picture] / Charles and Ray Eames. --
Santa Monica, Calif. : Pyramid Film Producers, distributor,
1978.
1 film reel (10 min.) : sd., b&w ; 16 mm.

Title and other information from distributor's catalogue.
Made in 1960?
Summary: Still pictures and quick cuts are used to present a
resumé of the popular music of the 1950's.

1. Music, Popular.   I. Eames, Charles.   II. Eames, Ray.

All information
from other
sources; source
given in note area

Date of
production
different from
date of release

Sample card 73
2nd level

792.2
R872

The Running jumping & standing still film [motion picture] /
thought by Spike Milligan ... [et al.] ; devised by Peter
Sellers ; directed by Dick Lester. -- [New York] : Janus
[distributor], 1959.
1 reel (11 min.) : sd., b&w ; 16 min. + 1 descriptive sheet.

Sepia print.
Summary: Members of the Goon Show troupe perform a series
of stunts in the style of the early silent comedies.

1. Comedy films.   I. Milligan, Spike.   II. Sellers, Peter.
III. Lester, Richard.

Sepia described
as black & white

784.4944   Sur le pont d'Avignon [motion picture] / par Le Trio lyrique ;
Su77   réalisation de J.P. Ladouceur et Wolf Koenig ; musique par
                Maurice Blackburn ; poupées de Gerald Budner et
                Blaikie-Morrison. -- Ottawa : l'Office national du film, 1951.
                1 film reel (5 min.) : sd., col. ; 16 mm. -- (Chansons de chez
       nous ; no 3)

                Summary: Puppets in medieval dress pantomine the old French
       folksong which describes the traffic over the bridge at Avignon.

                    (Continued on next card)

Sample card 74
2nd level

784.4944   Sur le pont d'Avignon [motion picture] ... 1951.   (Card 2)
Su77
                National Film Board of Canada: 106C-2051-033.

                1. Folk-songs, French.   2. Puppet films.

Sample card 74
(continued)

Producer's
number

GB   Dunes [motion picture] / filmed and edited by Fred Hudson ;
632   music by Michel Michelet ; produced by David Adams. --
D85   Santa Monica, Calif. : Pyramid Film Producers ; [New York] :
1968   distributed by Holt, Rinehart and Winston, [1968]
                1 film reel (7 min.) : sd., col. ; 16 mm.

                Distributed in Canada by: Toronto : International Telefilm
       Enterprises.
                Summary: A film without narration showing sand dunes and the
       life which inhabits them.

                1. Sand-dunes.   I. Hudson, Fred.

Sample card 75
3rd level

Compare with
NBM/1 s.c. 91

Local distribution
information in
note

Sample card 76
3rd level

M
1527
Y44

Yellow submarine [motion picture] / the Beatles ; directed by George Dunning ; screenplay by Lee Minoff ... [et al.] ; Jack Stokes and Robert Balser, animation directors. -- London : King Features [production company] ; [U.S.] : United Artists [distributor, 1968]
3 film reels (85 min.) : sd., col. ; 16 mm.

Credits: Editor, Brian J. Bishop ; musical director, George Martin ; voices, Paul Angelus, John Clive, Dick Emery, Geoff Hughes, Lance Percival.
From an original story by Lee Minoff.

(Continued on next card)

Sample card 76
(continued)

M
1527
Y44

Yellow submarine [motion picture] ... [1968]   (Card 2)

Based on a song by John Lennon and Paul McCartney.
Summary: An animated fantasy in which the Beatles perform many of their own songs while fighting off the Blue Meanies who menace the mythical realm of Sgt. Pepper's Lonely Hearts Club Band.

1. Animation (Cinematography)   2. Feature films.   3. Music, Popular.   I. Beatles.   II. Dunning, George.

Sample card 77
3rd level

Collective title

QL
49
D6
1970z

Dogs, cats & rabbits [motion picture]. -- [New York] : Texture Films, [197-]
1 film reel (8 min.) : sd., col. ; 16 mm.

Summary: Three separate filmmakers use different techniques to illustrate animal characteristics.
Contents: 41 barks / drawn & barked by Eliot Noyes, Jr. [U.S.] : Cyclops Films, 1972 -- Catsup / a film by Tana Hoban. [S.l.] : Tana Hoban, c1966 -- Rabbits, texture, shape, and fun / drawings by Bill Stitt ; movie, Walter K. Helmuth, Dick Blofson. [S.l. : s.n.], c1970.

(Continued on next card)

Contents note for individual works

Duration of individual works not easily ascertained

Sample card 77
(continued)

QL
49
D6
1970z

Dogs, cats & rabbits [motion picture] ... [197-] (Card 2)

1. Animation (Cinematography) 2. Children's films. 3. Cats.
4. Dogs. 5. Rabbits. I. Noyes, Eliot. 41 barks. II. Hoban,
Tana. Catsup. III. Stitt, Bill. Rabbits. IV. Title: 41 barks.
V. Title: Catsup. VI. Title: Rabbits.

Added entries for
each item of
contents.

Sample card 78
3rd level

BF
241
J32

Jackson, Alexander.
    Birth of a river [motion picture] : descent from the snow /
created by Alexander Jackson and Kenneth Osbourne. -- Boulder,
Colo. : Thorne Films [production company] ; Holyoke, Mass. :
Scott [distributor], c1970.
    1 film cartridge (Kodak) (2 min., 25 sec.) : si., col. ; super 8
mm.

    Notes on container. -- Summary: Colour, form, texture, and
photographic effects heighten visual awareness as melting mountain
snow becomes a river in the plains. -- Publisher's no.: 703.

    1. Rivers. 2. Visual perception. 3. Cinematography,
Abstract. I. Osbourne, Kenneth.

Entry under
personal name

Notes in
paragraph form

Silent motion
picture loop

Sample card 79
3rd level

PS
3531
.0733
G7
1903a

Porter, Edwin S.
    The great train robbery [motion picture] / written, directed,
photographed and edited by Edwin S. Porter. -- [West Orange,
N.J.] : Edison [production company], c1903 ; [Davenport, Iowa] :
Blackhawk Films [distributor]
    1 film reel (10 min.) : si., b&w with col. sequences ; standard
8 mm.

    Some scenes hand coloured in the 35 mm. print from which
this was made. -- Also available in 16 mm. -- Summary: One of
the first motion picture Westerns, using cross-editing techniques. --
Blackhawk: 865-35-1951.

(Continued on next card)

Entry under
personal name

Notes in
paragraph form
Available in two
formats
Silent standard 8
mm. motion
picture

PS
3531
.0733
G7
1903a

Porter, Edwin S. -- The great train robbery [motion picture] ...
c1903.   (Card 2)

1. Motion pictures, Silent.   2. Western films.   I. Title.

Pictures

Picture: a two-dimensional representation generally produced on an opaque backing.

Pictures, art reproductions, art prints, photographs, post cards, posters, reproductions of architectural renderings, and study prints are included under this heading and designated by the term "picture."

Pictures may be organized in a picture file (see pages 103 to 105). Items of permanent value to the collection should be completely catalogued for their effective use.

The general rules on pages 17 to 22 apply with the following additions and exceptions.

Sources of information
Information for the catalogue record is taken from the following sources in this order:

1. The item itself (Chief source of information). Preference is given to information on the picture rather than on the mount or frame;
2. Container;
3. Accompanying material;
4. Other sources.

Physical description area
Extent of item. List the number of art prints, art reproductions, photographs, pictures, postcards, posters, or study prints.

Option. List a more specific term (see sample card 84).

If an item has transparent overlays,[48] list the number in parentheses indicating the ones which are attached (see sample card 83).

Other physical details.
Art prints. List process and col., b&w, or sepia.
Art reproductions. List method of reproduction and b&w or col.
Photographs. If the photographic image is on transparent material, list "transparency" first in other physical details.
List negative (a positive print is not recorded).
List b&w or col.

Option. List the process.

Pictures, postcards, posters, study prints. List b&w or col.

Dimensions.
Art prints, art reproductions. Height × width of the item itself excluding mount or frame are listed in centimetres.
Photographs, pictures, postcards, posters, study prints. Height × width are listed in centimetres.

Note area
Art prints and art reproductions. If known, list information about original, such as location and size.

List unmounted or mounted, and details of mounting, if such information is useful (see sample card 80).

Care, handling, and storage
See General Guidelines for the Care, Handling, and Storage of Two-Dimensional, Opaque Materials on page 118.

```
759.4      Renoir, Auguste.
Ren            Les parapluies [picture]. -- Athena, 1975.
           1 art reproduction.

               Original in National Gallery, London.
               Unmounted.




               1. Impressionism (Art).   2. Painting, French.   I. Title.
```

Sample card 80[49]
1st level

Art reproduction

```
970.1      Indians of the eastern forests [picture]. -- Instructo Corp., c1968.
In2            11 pictures.

               Summary: Iroquois, Chippewa, and Seminole Indians are
           depicted in typical dress, shelter, activities, and environment.




               1. Chippewa Indians - Social life and customs.   2. Iroquois
           Indians - Social life and customs.   3. Seminole Indians - Social
           life and customs.
```

Sample card 81
1st level

Summary[50]
Picture

```
707        Surface [picture] / prepared by John Lidstone, editor-in-chief ;
Su77           Stanley T. Lewis, associate editor ; Sheldon Brody,
               photographic editor. -- New York : Reinhold, 1968.
               24 study prints : b&w and col. ; 61 × 46 cm. + 1 manual. --
           (Reinhold visuals : aids for art teaching ; portfolio 4)

               Partial contents: 1. Mustang Sally McBright / John Chamberlain
           -- 2. Geometry? / Joe Tilson -- 3. Between / Alfonso Ossorio --
           15. Sunflowers / Vincent van Gogh -- 24. Field painting / Jasper
           Johns.

                                         (Continued on next card)
```

Sample card 82[51]
2nd level

Series with
subtitle

Partial contents
note

Study print

707
Su77

Surface [picture] ... 1968.   (Card 2)

1. Art - Study and teaching.   I. Lidstone, John.   II. Lewis, Stanley T.   III. Brody, Sheldon.   IV. Series.

Sample card 82
(continued)

913
.377
H629

Historical reconstructions of Pompeii [picture] / produced by Encyclopaedia Britannica Films in collaboration with John W. Eadie. -- [Chicago] : Encyclopaedia Britanica Films, c1965. 4 study prints (1 attached overlay each) : col. ; 33 × 45 cm. + 1 teacher's study guide card. -- (History series)

Text on verso.
Contents: The House of the Faun -- The pistrinium (bakery) -- The theater -- The Temple of Apollo.

(Continued on next card)

Sample card 83
2nd level

Compare with
NBM/1 s.c. 101

Contents note
Study print

913
.377
H629

Historical reconstructions of Pompeii [picture] ... c1965.
    (Card 2)

1. Pompeii - Antiquities, Roman.   2. Architecture, Roman.

Sample card 83
(continued)

Sample card 84[52]
2nd level

```
581        Story of plant growth [picture]. -- Paoli, Pa. : Instructo Corp.,
.31          c1968.
St94         various flannel board pieces : col. + 1 teaching guide.




           1. Growth (Plants)   I. Title: Plant growth.
```

Flannel board

Sample card 85
3rd level

```
BF         Visual categories discovery set. No. 5 [picture]. -- Rochester,
241          N.Y. : Eastman Kodak [production company] ; Washington :
V58          Association for Educational Communications and Technology
             [distributor], c1969.
             50 photos. : col. ; 9 × 9 cm. + 1 teacher's note + 2 data
           collection sheets.

             Title from container.
             Data collection sheets intended to be duplicated for students.
             Summary: Miscellaneous photographs designed to develop visual
           literacy skills.

             1. Visual discrimination.
```

Statement of
function

Photograph

Realia

Realia: actual objects; artifacts, samples, specimens.

The general rules on pages 17 to 22 apply with the following additions and exceptions.

Publication, distribution, etc. area
List the place, publisher/producer/distributor and date for items which have been packaged or mounted by an outside agency (see sample card 88).

List only meaningful dates for all other realia (see sample card 86).

Physical description area
Extent of item. List the number and specific names of the item(s).

Other physical details. If appropriate, list material from which the object was made, the colour, and the method of preservation.[53]

Dimensions. If appropriate, list dimensions in centimetres with a word or phrase identifying the dimension.

When an item is packaged, list the type of package and its dimensions in centimetres.

Note area
Items which cannot be listed succinctly in the physical description area should be described more fully in the note area (see sample card 88).

Care, handling, and storage
See General Guidelines for the Storage of Three-Dimensional Media on page 118.

Sample card 86
1st level

```
391       [Mohawk Indian costume] [realia]. -- [186-?]
MOH          1 headdress, 1 beaded shirt, 1 pair of trousers, 1 pair of
          moccasins.

             Title supplied by cataloguer.



          1. Mohawk Indians - Costume and adornment.
```

Compare with
NBM/1 s.c. 104

597.53   [Sea-horses] [realia].
Se11   5 sea-horses : dried ; 6 cm. or smaller in vial, 8 cm. high.

          Title supplied by cataloguer.

       1. Sea-horse.

QE   Rocks and minerals [realia]. -- Fort Collins, Colo. : Scott
425   Scientific, 1973.
.4   15 samples ; in box, 14 × 9 × 2 cm. + 1 study guide ([29]
R62   p. ; 12 cm.)
1973

          List of composition and use on inside of container lid.
           Contents: Granite -- Gold ore -- Lepidolite -- Petrified wood --
Copper ore -- Flint -- Limestone -- Rose quartz -- Mica --
Uranium ore -- Fluorspar -- Feldspar -- Quartzite -- Sandstone --
Obsidian.

       1. Rocks.   2. Mineralogy.

Slides

Slide: a small unit of transparent material containing an image, mounted in rigid format and designed for use in a slide viewer or projector. Presentation of special slides in pairs (stereographs) produces a three-dimensional effect.

Slides and stereographs are included under this heading and designated by the term "slide."

Slides may be organized in slide trays (see pages 103 to 105). Items of permanent value to the collection should be completely catalogued for their effective use.

The general rules on pages 17 to 22 apply with the following additions and exceptions.

Sources of information
Information for the catalogue record should be taken from the following sources in this order:

1. The item itself. (Chief source of information). Preference is given to information on the slide rather than the mount;[54]
2. Container;
3. Accompanying material;
4. Other sources.

Physical description area
Extent of item.
    Slides. List the number of slides.
    Stereographs. List the number of stereographs. If the stereograph is circular, use the term "stereograph reel." The trade name or other technical specification and the number of double frames are added, each in its own parentheses.

Other physical details. If the sound is integral, list it.[55] Name the sound system in parentheses (see sample card 93).
    List b&w or col.

Dimensions.
    Slides. Height × width in centimetres are listed only if they are other than 5 × 5 cm.
    Stereographs. Dimensions are not listed.

Care, handling, and storage
See General Guidelines for the Care, Handling, and Storage of Film Media on page 116.

Sample card 89
1st level

709.02   Leonardo, da Vinci.
LEO   The Virgin Mary, the Child Jesus and St. Anne [slide]. --
      Blackhawk, [19--]
        1 slide. -- (Art treasures of the Louvre)

        1. Painting, Renaissance.   2. Christian art and symbolism.
    I. Title.   II. Series.

Single slide

QE   Glacial landforms [slide] / [presented by] National Film Board of
578   Canada and the Dept. of Energy, Mines and Resources ;
G53   director, F. Elliott ; executive producer, Hans Moller. --
         [Montreal] : N.F.B.C., c1970.
         46 slides : col.

         Technical consultants: Jack Ives, George Falconer.
         Date on film c1967.
         Manual (50 p. ; 20 cm.) by Jack Ives.

         1. Glacial landforms.   I. Canada. Dept. of Energy, Mines and
Resources.

Sample card 90[56]
3rd level

Compare with
NBM/1 s.c. 105

Slide set

557.1233 Jones, Bob.
J254   The Drumheller Badlands of Alberta [slide] / Bob Jones. --
         Toronto : Holt, Rinehart & Winston, c1972.
         12 slides : col. + 1 chart + 1 teacher's guide. -- (Holt
        geophotos resource kit ; 12)

         ISBN 0-03-925788-6 (unit 12). -- ISBN 0-03-925775-4 (kit).

         1. Geology - Drumheller (Alta.)   I. Title.

Sample card 91
2nd level

Item has 2 ISBNs

Slide set with 2
accompanying
materials

---

725   New York, Pennsylvania Station facade, 1906-1910 [slide]. --
P384   Toronto : United Church Pub. House, [19--]
         1 slide : glass, b&w ; 9 × 9 cm.

         1. Pennsylvania Station (New York, N.Y.).

Sample card 92[57]
2nd level

Dimensions other
than 5 × 5 cm.

Glass slide

Sample card 93
2nd level

617.158   [Lateral break in femur of human male] [slide] / Johns Hopkins
L345   University School of Medicine. -- [Baltimore, Md.] : The
          University, c1977.
          1 slide : sd. (3M Talking Slide), b&w

          Photographic reproduction of X-ray.
          Title supplied by cataloguer.

          1. Femur - Fracture.   I. Johns Hopkins University. School of
Medicine.

Sound slide

Sample card 94
1st level

531   Matter and energy [slide]. -- Viewmaster, c1969.
MAT   3 stereograph reels (Viewmaster) (7 double fr. each) + 1 story
          booklet.

Compare with
NBM/1 s.c. 108

          1. Force and energy.   2. Matter.

Stereograph

Sound Recordings

Sound recording: a recording on which sound vibrations have been registered by mechanical or electronic means so that the sound may be reproduced.

Discs, rolls, tapes (open reel-to-reel, cartridge, and cassette), sound pages, and sound recordings on film are included under this heading and designated by the term "sound recording."

The *Anglo-American Cataloguing Rules*, 2nd edition, chapter 6, should be consulted by those cataloguing sound track film, piano or organ rolls.

The general rules on pages 17 to 22 apply with the following additions and exceptions.

Sources of information

Information for the catalogue record should be taken from the following sources in this order:

1. The item itself (Chief source of information), e.g., the permanently affixed labels on discs, tape reels, cassettes, and cartridges;
2. Accompanying textual material;
3. Container;
4. Other sources.

If the item is comprised of parts which do not have a collective title, take the collective title from #2 or #3 above if one is found in these sources. Consider these as chief sources of information.

Main entry

1. The work(s) of one composer or author are entered under the name of that composer or author (see sample cards 101, 104, 108).
2. A sound recording which contains musical or literary works composed or written by two or more persons is entered under the principal performer, whether a person or a performing group, if up to three principal performers are given prominence in the chief source of information (see sample cards 100, 103, 106, 109, 111).
3. A sound recording which contains musical or literary works composed or written by two or more persons and has no principal performers or more than three principal performers is entered:
   (a) Under title, if the sound recording has a collective title for the component parts (see sample cards 112, 113);
   (b) Under the heading appropriate to the first work, e.g., that on side 1, band 1 of a sound disc, if the item does not have a collective title for the component parts (see sample card 110).
4. Items without a collective title may be described in either of two ways:
   a) As a unit (see sample card 103);
   b) In separate entries for each work. These entries are linked by a "With" note (see **Note area** below and sample cards 102A, 102B).

In both cases, main entry rules 1, 2, and 3 above are applied as appropriate. The call number selected for the item is that of the first work.

Uniform title

A uniform title is necessary to bring together various versions, editions, and arrangements of a work (see sample cards 98, 101, 102A, 102B, 105, 110, and non-musical work sample card 99).

Uniform titles are formulated according to the rules outlined in the *Anglo-American Cataloguing Rules*, 2nd edition, chapter 25.

Title and statement of responsibility area

Title proper and other title information. If the title of a work is a nondistinctive word or phrase, the medium of performance, key, opus number, etc. is listed as part of the title proper. If the title is distinctive, the medium of performance, key, opus number, etc. is listed as other title information.

Statement(s) of responsibility. Persons or groups are listed in this area if they are authors of spoken sound recordings, composers, collectors of field material, or persons who have contributed more to the recording than performance, execution, or interpretation. Those who function solely as performers, etc. are listed in the note area.

Publication, distribution, etc. area

Publisher, distributor, etc. If the item has both the name of the publisher and a subdivision with a distinctive name or trade name, list the subdivision or trade name rather than that of the parent company.

Physical description area

Extent of item. List the number of sound cartridges, sound cassettes, sound discs, sound tape reels, or sound pages.

> *Option*. If a general material designation is used, the word "sound" may be omitted from all specific material designations except "sound page" (see sample cards 98, 99, 106, 112).

List in parentheses after the specific material designation the total playing time stated on the item, its packaging, or its accompanying material. If duration is not stated, an approximate time, e.g., (ca. 30 min.), is listed if it can be ascertained easily.

Duration for an item without a collective title described as a unit (see **Main entry** 4(a) above) is listed in the note area. (See sample cards 101, 103.)

Other physical details.
> *Discs*. List playing speed in revolutions per minute (rpm).
> List groove characteristic only if it is not standard for the item.
> List mono., stereo., or quad., as appropriate.

> *Tapes*. List playing speed in inches per second (ips).
> List number of tracks only if it is not standard for the item.

List mono., stereo., or quad., as appropriate.
> *Option*. List recording and reproduction characteristics, e.g., NAB standard.

Sound pages. Other physical details are not given.

Dimensions.
> *Discs*. List the diameter in inches.

> *Tape reels*. List the diameter of the reel in inches.
> If the tape is other than 1/4 in., list the width in fractions of an inch.

> *Cassettes*. List the dimensions in inches only if they are other than $3^7/_8 \times 2^1/_2$ in.
> List the width of the tape in fractions of an inch only if it is other than $^1/_8$ in.

> *Cartridges*. List the dimensions in inches only if they are other than $5^1/_4 \times 7^7/_8$ in.
> List the width of the tape in fractions of an inch only if it is other than $^1/_4$ in.

> *Sound pages*. List height $\times$ width in centimetres.

Note area

List musical form if this information is not apparent in the rest of the description.

List performers and their medium of performance if not given elsewhere in the description, or if appropriate, combine these with a contents note.

List date of recording.

List any physical detail that is not standard to the item and affects its use.

List label name and publishers' numbers. If more than one number appears on the item, list the principal one. If this cannot be ascertained, list all numbers.

Added entries

Title added entries are never made for nondistinctive uniform titles which require the name of the composer for accurate identification, e.g., Scherzo, piano, op. 20, A major. (See also **References** below.)

If the work for which an added entry is made requires a uniform title, the uniform title must be used in the added entry (see sample cards 101, 103).

References

Because musical works appear under so many variant titles, composer/title *see* references must be made from well-known titles to the uniform title used, especially when the uniform title is in a language unfamiliar to the majority of the catalogue users:

Sample card 95

```
        Mozart, Wolfgang Amadeus.
          The magic flute

            SEE

        Mozart, Wolfgang, Amadeus.
          Die Zauberflöte




                        ◯
```

Title references can take the place of many added entries which would otherwise add unnecessary bulk to the catalogue:

Sample card 96

and/or

Sample card 97

```
        Die  Zauberflöte
      Mozart, Wolfgang, Amadeus.

        Editions of this work will be found under the composer's
        name.
```

```
            The magic flute
          Mozart, Wolfgang Amadeus.

            Editions of this work will be found under

          Mozart, Wolfgang Amadeus.
            Die Zauberflöte




                          ◯
```

Care, handling, and storage
See General Guidelines for the Care, Handling, and Storage of Magnetic Tape on page 117 and General Guidelines for the Care, Handling, and Storage of Sound Discs on page 117.

<table>
<tr><td>

782.8
SUL

</td><td>

Sullivan, Sir Arthur.
    [The Mikado. Sound recording]
    The Mikado / Gilbert and Sullivan. -- Richmond, [19--]
    2 discs.

    D'Oyly Carte Opera Company with chorus and orchestra conducted by Isidore Godfrey.
    Automatic sequence.
    Richmond: RS62004.

    1. Operas.   I. Gilbert, Sir William.   II. D'Oyly Carte Opera Company.   III. Title.

</td></tr>
</table>

Sample card 98
1st level

Single work

Duration not easily ascertained

Disc

<table>
<tr><td>

829
BEO

</td><td>

Beowulf. Sound recording.
    Beowulf and other Anglo-Saxon poetry. -- Caedmon, [1962]
    1 disc.

    Read in Old English by J.B. Bessinger, Jr.
    Anglo-Saxon text, in normalized orthography, by Francis P. Magoun, Jr., with English translation inserted.
    Caedmon: TC 1161.

    1. Anglo-Saxon poetry.   I. Bessinger, J.B.   II. Title.

</td></tr>
</table>

Sample card 99
1st level

Compare with NBM/1 s.c. 18

Uniform title as main entry

Disc with 1 accompanying material listed in note area

Sample card 100
2nd level

Entry under
performer

Collective title

Duration not
easily ascertained

```
784.947    Rebroff, Ivan.
R242           Kosaken müssen reiten [sound recording] : russische Leider in
           deutscher Sprache. -- [S.1.] : CBS, [19--]
               1 sound disc : 33¹/₃ rpm, stereo. ; 12 in.


               Subtitle on container: Russian songs in German.
               Ivan Rebroff, baritone.
               CBS: GS-90015.


               1. Songs, Russian.   I. Title.
```

Disc

Sample card 101
2nd level

No collective
title; works by 1
composer

```
785.6      Mendelssohn-Bartholdy, Felix.
M522           [Concertos, violin, orchestra, op. 64, E minor. Sound
           recording]
               Concerto in E minor, op. 64 ; Concerto in D minor (1822) /
           Mendelssohn. -- Hollywood, Calif. : Angel, c1972.
               1 sound disc : 33¹/₃ rpm, stereo. ; 12 in.


               The second work for violin and string orchestra.
               Yehudi Menuhin, violin ; London Symphony Orchestra, Rafael
           Frühbeck de Burgos, conductor.

                                              (Continued on next card)
```

Sample card 101
(continued)

```
785.6      Mendelssohn-Bartholdy, Felix. -- [Concertos, violin, orchestra, op.
M522           64, E minor] ... c1972.   (Card 2)


               Durations: 27 min. ; 22 min.
               Programme notes on container.
               Angel: 536850.


               1. Concertos (Violin)   2. Concertos (Violin with string
           orchestra)   I. Mendelssohn-Bartholdy, Felix. Concertos, violin,
           string orchestra, D minor. II. Menuhin, Yehudi. III. Frühbeck de
           Burgos, Rafael. IV. London Symphony Orchestra.
```

Disc

785.7471   Mozart, Wolfgang Amadeus.
M877   [Quartets, strings, no. 19, K. 465, C major. Sound recording]
       Quartet no. 19 in C major, K. 465 ("Dissonant") / Mozart. --
Hollywood, Calif. : Seraphim, [1970]
       on 1 side of 1 sound disc (24 min.) : 33¹/₃ rpm, stereo. ;
12 in.

       Drolč Quartet.
       Programme notes on container.
       Seraphim: s-60137.

                                   (Continued on next card)

Sample card
102A
2nd level

No collective
title, works by
different
composers
catalogued
separately

Disc

785.7471   Mozart, Wolfgang Amadeus. -- [Quartets, string, no. 19, K. 465,
M877   C major. Sound recording] ... [1970]   (Card 2)

       With: Quartet no. 77 in C, op. 76, no. 3 ("Emperor") /
Haydn.

       1. String quartets - To 1800.   I. Drolč-Quartett.

Sample card
102A
(continued)

785.7471   Haydn, Joseph.
M877   [Quartets, strings, no. 78, op. 76, no. 3, C major. Sound
recording]
       Quartet no. 77 in C, op. 76, no. 3 ("Emperor") / Haydn. --
Hollywood, Calif. : Seraphim, [1970]
       on 1 side of 1 sound disc (28 min.) : 33¹/₃ rpm, stereo. ;
12 in.

       Drolč Quartet.
       Programme notes on container.
       Seraphim: S-60137.
       With: Quartet no. 19 in C major, K. 465 ("Dissonant") /
Mozart.

       1. String quartets - To 1800.   I. Drolč-Quartett.

Sample card
102B
2nd level

No collective
title, works by
different
composers
catalogued
separately

Disc

Sample card 103
2nd level

785.7471   Drolč-Quartett.
D835   Quartet no. 19 in C major, K. 465 ("Dissonant") / Mozart.
       Quartet no. 77 in C, op. 76, no. 3 ("Emperor") / Haydn [sound
       recording]. -- Hollywood, Calif. : Seraphim, [1970]
         1 sound disc : 33⅓ rpm, stereo. ; 12 in.

         Drolč Quartet. -- Durations: 24 min. ; 28 min. -- Programme
       notes on container. -- Seraphim: S-60137.

         1. String quartets - To 1800.   I. Mozart, Wolfgang Amadeus.
       Quartets, strings, no. 19, K. 465, C major.   II. Haydn, Joseph.
       Quartets, strings, no. 78, op. 76, no. 3, C major.

No collective
title, works by
different
composers
catalogued as a
unit

Notes in one
paragraph

Disc

Sample card 104
3rd level

B   Thoreau, Henry David.
931   An interview with Henry David Thoreau [sound recording] /
T4   edited by Thomas M. Johnson. -- Glenview, Ill. : Scott,
I5   Foresman, c1964.
1964   1 sound disc (30 min.) : 33⅓ rpm, mono. ; 12 in. + 1
       filmstrip (111 fr. : col. ; 35 mm.) + 1 reading script (8 p. ;
       31 cm.)

        Disc has automatic advance signals only.
        Summary: Excerpts from Thoreau's writings read by Hans
      Conried in answer to questions of a present day student.
      Illustrated with pictures of Walden and the Thoreau Memorial.

                  (Continued on next card)

Compare with
NBM/1 s.c. 20

Disc with two
accompanying
materials

Sample card 104
(continued)

B   Thoreau, Henry David. -- An interview with Henry David Thoreau
931   [sound recording] ... c1964.   (Card 2)
T4
I5   Scott, Foresman: XCTV 97108-97109.
1964

        1. Johnson, Thomas M.   II. Title.

M
1505
C37
H3
	Caravan Stage Company.
	    [Hands up. Selections. Sound recording]
	    CP transcontinental ; Somebody robbed the CPR ; Bill Miner
	song / Caravan Stage Company. -- Vernon, B.C. (Fintry RR7) :
	CSC, c1977.
	    1 sound disc (8 min.) : 45 rpm, mono. ; 7 in.
	
	    CSC 07, 08.
	
	    1. Musical reviews, comedies, etc. - Excerpts. I. Title: Hands
	up [sound recording]

Sample card 105
3rd level

Work where the activity of
the group went beyond
performance

Address of publisher not
likely to be listed
elsewhere

General material
designation used in title
added entry. See page 12
for explanation

Disc

784
MIL
	Mills Brothers.
	    The Mills Brothers' great hits [sound recording]. -- Dot, 1958.
	    1 cassette (ca. 60 min.)
	
	    Songs performed by the Mills Brothers.
	    Dot: CS 25157.
	
	    1. Music, Popular (Songs, etc.) I. Title.

Sample card 106
1st level

Compare with
NBM/1 s.c. 32 &
33

Entry under
performing group

Cassette

Z
696
D82
1977
	Centennial of the Dewey decimal classification [sound recording].
	    -- Chicago : American Library Association, c1977.
	    1 sound cassette (88 min.) : 3³/₄ ips, mono.
	
	    Recorded at the 100th anniversary annual ALA conference,
	July, 1976, Resources and Technical Services Division programme.
	    Contents: Mr. Dewey's classification, Mr. Cutter's catalog, and
	Dr. Hitchcock's chickens / Phyllis A. Richmond -- DC outward /
	Richard B. Sealock -- DC inward / Benjamin A. Custer.
	    ALA: 76-15.
	
	    1. Classification, Dewey decimal. I. American Library
	Association. Conference (95th : 1976 : Chicago)

Sample card 107
3rd level

Collective title

Cassette

819.1　　Waddington, Miriam.
W117　　　　Miriam Waddington [sound recording]. -- Toronto : Ontario
Institute for Studies in Education, [1969]
　　　　　　1 sound tape reel (30 min.) : 7¹/₂ ips, mono. ; 6 in. --
(Canadian poets on tape)

　　　　　　Summary: Readings of the poet's own works published between
1945-1969.

　　　　　　I. Ontario Institute for Studies in Education.　　II. Series.

Sample card 108
2nd level

No order number
on tape

Reel-to-reel tape

784　　　Bramlett, Bonnie.
B732　　　　Lady's choice [sound recording]. -- Macon, Ga. : Capricorn,
c1976.
　　　　　　1 sound recording (36 min.)

　　　　　　Vocalist: Bonnie Bramlett.
　　　　　　Available on disc or cassette.
　　　　　　Capricorn: CP 0169 (disc), M5 0169 (cassette)

　　　　　　1. Music, Popular (Songs, etc.)　　I. Title.

Sample card 109[58]
2nd level

Entry under
performer

Available in two
formats

M　　　Verdi, Giuseppe.
1505　　　[Aida. Celeste Aida. Sound recording]
V473　　　Celeste Aida / Verdi.　Papagena! Papegena! / Mozart.
A5　　　Selections from Billy Budd / Britten. -- [S.1., s.n.], 1975
(London : Apex Sound)
　　　　　　1 sound cartridge : 3³/₄ ips, mono.

　　　　　　Sung in English with piano accompaniment.
　　　　　　Sheila Miller, soprano ; Jean Scott, contralto ; John Green,
tenor ; Peter Paul, baritone ; Noel Stringer, piano.
　　　　　　Durations: 9 min. ; 8 min. ; 12 min.

　　　　　　1. Operas - Excerpts.　　I. Mozart, Wolfgang Amadeus. Die
Zauberflöte. Papagena! Papagena!　　II. Britten, Benjamin. Billy
Budd. Selections.

Sample card 110
3rd level

No collective title
and more than 3
principal
performers

No publisher;
manufacturer
given

Durations for
individual works

Cartridge

Sample card 111
3rd level

```
M          Houston, Thelma.
1497           I've got the music in me [sound recording]. -- Santa Barbara,
H68        Calif. : Sheffield Lab, c1975.
I8             1 sound disc : 33¹/₃ rpm, stereo. ; 12 in.
1975
               Thelma Houston & Pressure Cooker. -- Direct to disc
           recording. -- Contents: I've got the music in me -- Reggae time
           -- To know you is to love you -- Pressure cooker -- Don't
           misunderstand -- Step in time -- Dish rag -- Got to get you into
           my life. -- Sheffield: SL7/SL8.

               1. Music, Popular (Songs, etc.)   I. Pressure Cooker.
           II. Title.
```

Entry under 1st
listed performer

Notes in one
paragraph

Contents note

Disc

Sample card 112
1st level

```
782.8      Stars of the silver screen 1929-1930 [sound recording]. -- RCA
STA            Victor, [1967]
               1 disc (48 min.)

               16 songs from 16 motion pictures by 15 performers and
           1 performing group.
           RCA Victor: LPV 538.

               1. Motion pictures - Songs and music.
```

Collective title
and no principal
performer

Disc

Sample card 113
2nd level

```
783.4      The French ars antiqua [sound recording]. -- New York :
F889           Lyrichord, c1960.
               1 sound disc : 33¹/₃ rpm, stereo. ; 12 in. + 1 text ([6] p. ;
           26 cm.). -- (Music of the Middle Ages. Vol. 7, The thirteenth
           century) (Expériences anonymes series)

               Russell Oberlin, countertenor ; Charles Bressler, Robert Price,
           tenors ; Gordon Meyers, baritone ; Martha Blackman, viol.
           Programme notes by William C. Waite on container.

                                              (Continued on next card)
```

Collective title
and more than 3
principal
performers

Series and
subseries and
more than 1
series statement

Disc

Sample card 113
(continued)

783.4   The French ars antiqua [sound recording] ... c1960.   (Card 2)
F889

      1. Part-songs, Sacred - To 1800.   2. Part-songs, French - To
1800.   I. Oberlin, Russell.   II. Bressler, Charles.   III. Price,
Robert.   IV. Meyers, Gordon.   V. Blackman, Martha.
VI. Series.

Sample card 114[59]
2nd level

510   Concepts in mathematics [sound recording] / developed by
C744   U-SAIL, Utah System Approach to Individual Learning. -- St.
Paul, Minn. : 3M, c1974.
      54 sound pages (ca. 216 min.) ; 30 × 22 cm. + 1 teacher's
guide.

      For 3M Sound Page player.
      Audience level: Grades 4-6.

      1. Mathematics.   I. Utah System Approach to Individualized
Learning.

Sound page

Technical Drawings[60]

Technical drawing: a plan, elevation, cross section, detail, diagram, perspective, etc., made for use in an engineering, architectural, or other technical context.

The general rules on pages 17 to 22 apply with the following additions and exceptions.

Sources of information
Information for the catalogue record is taken from the following sources in this order:

1. The item itself (Chief source of information). If there is more than one title on the item, preference should be given to information in the title block;
2. Container;
3. Accompanying material;
4. Other sources.

Edition area
List the statement from a drawing which indicates a particular edition. Examples of such phrases are "tender drawing," "contract drawing," "as built drawing."

Publication, distribution, etc. area
There are few technical drawings marketed by commercial producers. Most drawings are produced by the firm or individual responsible for their creation. While the firm or individual may sell the drawings in some instances, they do not constitute a publisher/distributor. The rules for Locally-Produced, Non-Commercial Materials on page 99 should be used for this area, when appropriate.

Date. List date of the latest revision. For a sounding survey drawing list the date of sounding.

Physical description area
Extent of item. List the number of technical drawings using a specific term, such as structural sketch, mechanical drawing. In cataloguing a set the component parts are listed in the following order: architectural, structural, mechanical, electrical, specialized drawings.

Other physical details. List the method of reproduction or the material of the drawing, whichever term or phrase indicates whether a drawing can be reproduced. For example, the terms "mylar," "tracing paper," and "white linen" indicate reproducible drawings, while "whiteprints," "blueprints," and "blue linen" are not reproduced easily.

Dimensions. List height × width of the drawing measured from the inside border. If the drawing is folded, list these dimensions also.

Note area
List the scale in the terms used on the drawing(s). If the scales in a set vary, use the term "scales vary" or list the range of scales.

List date of original drawing if different from the date in the publication/distribution, etc. area. If the drawing was originally produced and revised in the same year and the media centre's patrons find this information valuable, the month may be added before the date in both the publication/distribution area and the note area.

List autopositive or vandyke, if appropriate.

Care, handling, and storage
See General Guidelines for the Care, Handling, and Storage of Two-Dimensional, Opaque Materials on page 118.

725   Government of Canada building, Toronto (North York) Ontario
GOV   [technical drawing] / Dubois, Strong, Bindhardt ... [et al.]. --
        As built drawings. -- 1978.
        70 architectural drawings.

        Scale varies.

        1. North York (Ont.) - Public buildings.   I. Dubois, Strong,
Bindhardt (Firm)

Sample card 115
1st level

725.6   Kingston Regional Reception Centre alteration [to] heating [system]
K619   [technical drawing] / Public Works Canada. -- 1971.
        1 mechanical drawing : tracing paper ; 60 × 90 cm. folded to
30 × 45 cm.

        Scale $1/8$ in. to 1 ft.

        1. Prisons - Kingston (Ont.) - Heating and ventilation.
I. Canada. Dept. of Public Works.

Sample card 116
2nd level

Words added to
make title more
understandable

WX   Greater Vancouver Regional Hospital Laundry [technical drawing] /
165   Quan, Carruthers, King & Quan Consultants Ltd. [prime
G74   consultants] ... [et al.]. -- Tender drawings. -- 1979.
        6 architectural drawings, 2 structural drawings, 6 mechanical
drawings, 5 electrical drawings, 4 process drawings : whiteprints ;
87 × 113 cm. folded to 22 × 29 cm.

        Scales vary from 1:50 to 1:200.

        1. Laundries, Hospital.   I. Quan, Carruthers, King & Quan
Consultants.

Sample card 117
3rd level

National Library
of Medicine
classification

Transparencies

Transparency: an image produced on transparent material, designed for use with an overhead projector.

Transparencies may be organized as ephemeral materials (see pages 103 to 105). Items of permanent value to the collection should be completely catalogued for their effective use.

The general rules on pages 17 to 22 apply with the following additions and exceptions.

Sources of information
Information for the catalogue record should be taken from the following sources in this order:

1. The item itself (Chief source of information). Preference is given to information on the transparency rather than on the mount;[61]
2. Container;
3. Accompanying material;
4. Other sources.

Physical description area
Extent of item. List the number of transparencies and, if applicable, following in parentheses the number of overlays. Attached overlays are indicated.

Other physical details. List b&w or col.

Dimensions. Height × width of the item itself excluding mount are listed in centimetres.

Care, handling, and storage
See General Guidelines for the Care, Handling, and Storage of Film Media on page 116. Additional storage suggestions for transparencies will be found under General Guidelines for the Care, Handling, and Storage of Two-Dimensional Opaque Materials on page 118.

```
611        The Brain [transparency]. -- Instructo Corp., c1967.
BRA        1 transparency (5 attached overlays)




.




           1. Brain - Anatomy.
```

551.6971   Climate and weather [transparency] = Climats. -- [Montreal] :
C613   National Film Board of Canada, c1969.
           1 transparency (3 overlays) : col. ; 19 × 25 cm. --
           (Geographical maps of Canada = Cartes géographiques du Canada)

        1. Canada - Climate.   I. Title: Climats.   II. Series.

Sample card 119
2nd level

Compare with
NBM/1 s.c. 113

Parallel title
proper & series
title

551.6   Shirley, Robert T.
Sh66   Understanding climate and weather [transparency] / written and
          narrated by Robert T. Shirley. -- Chicago : Weber Costello,
          c1971.
           6 transparencies (2 attached overlays each) : col. ; 21 × 27
          cm. + 1 sound disc + 1 teacher's manual.

          Contents: 1. Latitude -- 2. Land forms -- 3. Elevation --
      4. Body of water -- 5. Winds -- 6. Ocean currents.

        1. Meteorology.   I. Title.

Sample card 120
2nd level

Transparency
with 2
accompanying
materials

QC   Electricity & magnetism. Series EM-A [transparency]. -- King of
523   Prussia, Pa. : Photo Motion, c1972.
E44   12 transparencies : col. ; 21 × 26 cm. + 1 syllabus (2 p. ;
          27 cm.)

          Designed for Photo Motion Activator which creates animation.
          Summary: Basic elements of electrical science including static
      electricity, Van de Graaff generator, cells, electrolysis of water,
      electroplating, circuits, electrical resistance, and electromotive
      force.

        1. Electricity.   2. Magnetism.

Sample card 121
3rd level

Animated
transparency

Videorecordings

Videorecording: a recording designed for television playback on which both pictures and sound have been registered electronically.

Reel-to-reel tapes, cartridges, cassettes, and discs are included under this heading and designated by the term "videorecording."

Videotapes which must be, or will be, erased after a limited time do not merit the expense of full cataloguing. They can be listed in subject bibliographies which may be posted near the catalogue. Items of permanent value to the collection should be completely catalogued for their effective use.

The rules for Motion Pictures on pages 64 to 70 apply to videorecordings with the following additions and exceptions.

Sources of information
Some recordings of broadcast television programmes may display the series title only. The title and/or statement of responsibility are presented orally; these oral statements are used in the absence of a written title as supplied information (see sample card 129).

Physical description area
Extent of item. List the number of videocartridges, videocassettes, videodiscs, or videoreels.

> *Option*. If a general material designation is used, the prefix "video" may be omitted from the specific material designation (see sample cards 122, 123A, 123B).

List in its own parentheses after the specific material designation, any technical specification, such as a trade name, which is necessary information for the use of the item. If the item is available in the media centre in more than one video format the technical specifications are listed in the note area (see sample card 124 and note on page 126).

List in its own parentheses the total playing time in minutes. If appropriate, the duration of parts of an item with the same or almost the same playing time is listed as "(10 min. each)." If no duration is stated on the item, list an approximate time if this can be ascertained readily.

Other physical details. List sound and b&w or col.
    Videodiscs. List playing speed in revolutions per minute.

Dimensions.
    Videotapes. List width in inches.
    Videodiscs. List diameter in inches.

Note area
See page 64 for rules covering featured performers and other participants, date of original production, and country of original release.

List colour recording system if a media centre's holdings are to be used internationally.

List the videorecording system, if it has not been listed in the physical description area. The notes "U standard" or "Beta" may be used in this area rather than listing a specific system in the extent of item if the format, e.g., Sony U-Matic or Betamax, is one which is compatible with other manufacturers (see sample card 125).

> *Videotapes*. List the line and field standards and the modulation frequency for two-inch videotapes.
> List the generation of copy and whether a master or show copy.

Care, handling, and storage
Videotapes. See General Guidelines for the Care, Handling, and Storage of Magnetic Tape on page 117.

Videodiscs. The manufacturer's advertisements emphasize the durability of videodiscs. They appear to require no special care for normal media centre handling and storage.

<table>
<tr><td>

812
WIL

Wilder, Thornton.
   Infancy ; Childhood [videorecording]. -- National Educational Television, 1970.
   1 reel (Shibaden SV-727) (90 min.) : sd., b&w ; 1 in. -- (Playhouse. A Generation of leaves)

   Cast: Fred Gwynne, Eileen Brennan.
   Summary: Two one-act serio-comic plays about the failure of generations to communicate.

   I. Title. II. Title: Childhood. III. Series.

</td></tr>
</table>

Sample card 122
1st level

Compare with
NBM/1 s.c. 115

Item without a
collective title
described as a
unit

Subseries

Videotape

<table>
<tr><td>

770.28
PHO

The Photographic model [videorecording]. -- CTV, 1970.
   on 1 reel (Panasonic NV 504) (30 min.) : sd., b&w ; 1 in. -- (University of the air. Photography ; pt. 3)

   Summary: Illustrates the correct way to arrange a photographic set; model posture; grooming; posing, etc.
   With: Color photography.

   1. Models, Fashion. 2. Photography - Technique. I. Series.

</td></tr>
</table>

Sample card 123A[62]
1st level

Compare with
NBM/1 s.c. 119

Item without a
collective title,
the parts
catalogued
separately

Videotape

<table>
<tr><td>

770.28
PHO

Color photography [videorecording]. -- CTV, 1970.
   on 1 reel (Panasonic NV 504) (30 min.) : sd., b&w ; 1 in. -- (University of the air. Photography ; pt. 5)

   Summary: Reviews primary and secondary colours and those compositional factors relating primarily to colour photography.
   With: The Photographic model.

   1. Colour photography. I. Series.

</td></tr>
</table>

Sample card 123B
1st level

Compare with
NBM/1 s.c. 120

Item without a
collective title,
the parts
catalogued
separately

Videotape

020.75   Landon, Richard.
L236u   [Rare books, collecting, libraries, and trade] [videorecording]. --
          Toronto : OECA, c1977.
              1 videorecording (30 min.) : sd., b&w. -- (Speaking of books
          with Robert Fulford).

              Title supplied by cataloguer.
020.75   Available in media centre as Sony U-Matic or Sony AV ½ in.
L236h   Summary: Robert Fulford interviews R. Landon, head of the
          Thomas Fisher Rare Book Library, University of Toronto, about
          book collecting, the rare book trade, and the resources of the
          library.

                                           (Continued on next card)

2 formats
available

020.75   Landon, Richard. -- [Rare books, collecting, libraries, and trade]
L236u   [videorecording] ... c1977.   (Card 2)

              1. Bibliography - Rare books.   2. Book collecting.
          I. Fulford, Robert.   II. Thomas Fisher Rare Book Library.

Z   Austin, Derek.
695   An introduction to PRECIS indexing [videorecording] / Derek
92   Austin. -- [College Park, Md.] : Library Training Consultants,
A86   c1977.
              2 videocassettes (ca. 56 min. each) : sd., b&w ; ¾ in. + 1
          workshop handout (12 leaves ; 28 cm.)

              Recorded at the International PRECIS Workshop, October 19,
          1976, sponsored by the College of Library and Information
          Services, University of Maryland.
              U standard.

                                           (Continued on next card)

Cassette

```
Z          Austin, Derek. -- An introduction to PRECIS indexing
695            [videorecording] ... c1977.   (Card 2)
92
A86




              1. PRECIS (Indexing system)   I. International PRECIS
           Workshop (1976 : University of Maryland)

                              ◯
```

```
398.2      The Slipper and the rose [videorecording] : the story of
S ℓ37          Cinderella / music and lyrics, Richard M. Sherman and Robert
               B. Sherman ; directed by Bryan Forbes ; produced by Stuart
               Lyons. -- Universal City, Calif. : MCA, [1978]
               3 videodiscs (Discovision) (127 min.) : sd., col., 1800 rpm ;
           12 in.

               Reproduction of original feature film: London : Paradine
           Co-Productions, c1976.
               Cast: Richard Chamberlain, Gemma Craven, Annette Crosbie,
           Edith Evans, Christopher Gable, Michael Hornden, Margaret
           Lockwood, Kenneth More.
                              ◯
                                        (Continued on next card)
```

Videodisc

```
398.2      The Slipper and the rose [videorecording] ... [1978]   (Card 2)
S ℓ37
               Credits: Screenplay, Bryan Forbes, Richard M. Sherman, Robert
           B. Sherman.
               Summary: A musical retelling and modernization of the fairy
           tale.

               1. Fairy tales.   2. Feature films.   3. Musical revues,
           comedies, etc.   I. Forbes, Bryan.   II. Sherman, Richard M.
           III. Sherman, Robert B.   IV. Chamberlain, Richard.
           V. Craven, Gemma.   VI. Title: Cinderella.

                              ◯
```

Locally-Produced, Noncommercial Materials[64]

A media centre's collection may include locally-produced, noncommercial materials. These may be unique materials donated by a patron, such as oral history recordings, or items which are produced by the students or staff of, and for use in, an institution. If such materials are expected to have a long term use, they should be catalogued. Because many of these materials are inadequately labelled, much of the cataloguing information will be supplied by the cataloguer. Information taken from other than the primary sources is enclosed in square brackets. Other sources of information can be:

1. The content, e.g., the main entry and title in sample card 129 are derived from the introduction made verbally at the beginning of the tape. The title on sample card 128 was taken from a label, the statement of responsibility from the text. Both author and title were listed

on the label attached to the sample card 130 item.

2. The donor, who is frequently also the producer, e.g., the Grade 6 teacher supplied the information on sample card 127.

Publication, distribution, etc. area
If the "author" is also responsible for the manufacture of the item and is named in the statement of responsibility, the name, together with the place, is not repeated in the publication/distribution area.

If the "author" is not responsible for the production or manufacture of the item, the name of the manufacturer is given in parentheses following the date (see sample card 129).

Date. The date of manufacture is listed. For nonprocessed sound recordings, the date of recording is given in the note area (see sample card 130).

```
                                                          Sample card 127
                                                          1st level


623      [British fort in North America, ca. 1700] [model] / [Woodland
BRI       Public School Grade 6 class]. -- [1978]
          1 model (wood and cardboard)

          Title supplied by cataloguer.




          1. Fortification.    2. North America - Defenses - History.        Model
                              O
```

791.4309   Hofbauer, Ruth.
09353   The woman's motion picture film kit [kit] / Ruth Hofbauer,
H673   Freda Dunham. -- [1977?]
          3 pamphlets, 16 pictures on 15 sheets, 3 posters, 47 slides,
     2 sound cassettes, 1 text ; in container, 26 × 48 × 24 cm.

         1. Women in motion pictures.   I. Dunham, Freda.   II. Title.

Sample card 128[65]
2nd level

Kit

Z   Halpenny, Francess G.
481   Problems in Canadian publishing [videorecording] : a lecture. --
H3   [1972] (Willowdale, Ont. : Seneca College Instructional Media
      Dept.)
         1 videoreel (Sony EV-320) (45 min.) : sd., b&w ; 1 in.

      Title supplied from oral introduction.
      Master copy.

         1. Publishers and publishing - Canada.

Sample card 129
3rd level

Videotape

FC   Stewart, Jean, 1888-
3095   Pioneer days in Bruce County [sound recording] / Jean Stewart.
B78   2 sound tape reels (ca. 100 min.) : 7$^{1}/_{2}$ ips, 2 track, mono. ;
S7   5 in.

      Recorded in 1978.
      With undated map: Early pioneer settlements, Bruce Country.
      Summary: Mrs. Stewart recounts tales about the first settlers in
    Bruce County, Ont., told to her by her mother and grandmother.

         1. Pioneers - Bruce County (Ont.)   I. Title.   II. Title: Early
    pioneer settlements, Bruce County [map].

Sample card 130
3rd level

Date added to
main entry to
distinguish from
others of the
same name

No collective
title; one work
clearly
predominant

Sound tape

References to Materials
Not Listed in the Catalogue

3

Ephemeral Materials, Vertical Files, and Picture Files

Not all media centre materials warrant the expenditure involved in complete cataloguing and processing. The media specialist must decide whether the format of the material is durable enough to withstand normal use and whether the content of the material is valuable enough to add to the centre's permanent collection. Newspaper clippings, pamphlets, single unmounted pictures and sketches, and charts and plans of curricular or local interest are among the materials generally considered ephemeral.

Ephemeral materials should be organized economically with a minimum of cataloguing, yet in a manner which will ensure their easy retrieval.

This can be effected by placing these materials in a vertical file and indexing them by one of the following methods:

1. For a particular item, the appropriate heading is selected from the subject heading list used for other media centre materials. The item is placed in a file folder labelled with this subject heading, and the folder is filed alphabetically in the vertical file. Directions for the retrieval of items are filed under the appropriate heading in the catalogue. The following may be used as a guide.

Sample card 131

VOLCANOES

    Additional material on this subject will be found in the vertical file under the above heading.

2. For a particular item, the appropriate classification number is selected from the classification scheme used for other media centre materials. The item is placed in a file folder labelled with this number, and the folder is filed numerically in the vertical file. Directions for the retrieval of items are filed under the appropriate heading in the catalogue. The following may be used as a guide.

Sample card 132

```
┌──────────────────────────────────────────┐
│ VOLCANOES                                │
│                                          │
│    Additional material on this subject will be found in the │
│    vertical file under 551.21            │
│                                          │
│                                          │
│                     ◯                    │
└──────────────────────────────────────────┘
```

Items of permanent value to the collection should be completely catalogued for their effective use. However, if a media centre has a small staff with limited time to devote to cataloguing, some media, e.g., picture sets, study prints, transparencies, single slides, art prints, and maps, may be organized informally. The following may be used as a guide.

Sample card 133

```
┌──────────────────────────────────────────┐
│ VOLCANOES                                │
│                                          │
│    Additional material on the above subject will be found in the │
│    special collections indicated below   │
│                                          │
│    ☐ Vertical file      ☐ Slide trays    │
│                                          │
│    ☐ Map drawer         ☐ Art collection │
│                                          │
│    ☐ Picture file       ☐                │
│                                          │
│                     ◯                    │
└──────────────────────────────────────────┘
```

Media centres with intershelved, uncatalogued
materials may use the following as a guide.

VOLCANOES

    Additional material on this subject will be found on the
shelves following other materials numbered 551.21

Sample card 134

References to In-Depth Indexing

Many media centres have various indexes and lists to supplement the main catalogue. These specialized lists, often computer-produced, include analytics and other in-depth indexing in certain subject fields. The public catalogue should direct the patron's attention to the existence of such lists. The following may be used as a guide.

Sample card 135

Beethoven, Ludwig van.

    SEE ALSO   Sound Disc Catalogue at the Information Desk for other recordings of works by this composer.

Sample card 136

PANCREAS

    Additional information on this subject will be found by consulting special lists in the departments indicated below

    ☐ Government Publications Division

    ☐ Medical Division Library

    ☐ Serials Division

    ☐ Science Division

Glossary and Abbreviations

4

Glossary

The definitions in this glossary have been constructed for descriptive cataloguing purposes only. Definitive technical descriptions have not been attempted. General material designations from the North American list are indicated in bold face.

Aperture card *see* **Microform**

Architectural rendering — A pictorial representation of a building before it has been built, intended to show how the building will look when completed. *See* **Art original; Picture.**

Art original — An original two- or three-dimensional work of art.

Art print *see* **Picture**

Art reproduction *see* **Model; Picture**

Artifact *see* **Realia**

Audiodisc *see* **Sound recording**

Audiorecord *see* **Sound recording**

Audioroll *see* **Sound recording**

Audiotape *see* **Sound recording**

Audiowire *see* **Sound recording**

Cartographic material *see* **Globe; Map**

Cartridge — An enclosed container for film or magnetic tape in an endless loop format.

Cassette — An enclosed container for film or magnetic tape in reel-to-reel format.

Chart — A sheet of information arranged in tabular or graphic form produced on an opaque backing.

Chart (Cartography) — A map designed for special purposes, e.g., aeronautics, navigation, etc.

Chief source of information — The source of bibliographic data to be given first preference as the source from which information for a bibliographic record is taken.

Collective title — The inclusive title for an item containing several works.

Data set name — In certain computer systems, the name that the software recognizes as the identifier of a machine readable data file.

Diorama — A scene produced in three dimensions by placing objects, figures, etc., in front of a representational background.

Distributor — An agent or agency holding exclusive or shared rights for the marketing of an item.

Filmloop *see* **Motion picture**

Filmslip *see* **Filmstrip**

Filmstrip — A roll of film containing a succession of images designed to be viewed one frame at a time. A short length of such film, sometimes mounted in a rigid format, is called a filmslip.

Flash card — A card printed with words, numerals, or pictures, designed for rapid identification.

Game — A set of materials designed for play according to prescribed rules.

General material designation — The term used to classify the type of material to which an item belongs, e.g., **Picture.**

Globe — A sphere representing the earth, other celestial bodies, or the universe.

Graph *see* **Chart**

Internal user label — A machine-readable identifier which often provides data about the contents of a machine-readable data file.

International standard book number *see* Standard number

International standard serial number *see* Standard number

Kit — A set of material composed of many textual parts, or, two or more media none of which is identifiable as the predominant constituent of the item.

Laboratory kit *see* **Kit**

Map — A flat representation of part or all of either the earth or the universe. Includes the following format: Relief model.

Microform — A miniature reproduction of printed or other graphic matter which cannot be utilized without magnification. Includes the following formats:

> *Aperture card* — A card with an opening or openings within which a microform is mounted.
> *Microfiche* — A microform on a flat sheet of film.
> *Microfilm* — A microform on a roll of film.
> *Microopaque* — A microform on opaque material.

Microscope slide — A specialized slide produced specifically for use with a microscope or microprojector.

Mock-up *see* **Model**

Model — A three-dimensional representation of

an object, either exact or to scale; a mock-up.

Motion picture loop *see* **Motion picture**

Motion picture — Film, with or without sound, bearing a sequence of images which create the illusion of movement when projected.

Object program — The computer language program created by the compiler of the source program of a machine readable data file.

Overhead projectual *see* **Transparency**

Overlay — A transparent sheet designed to be superimposed on another sheet for modification of the original data.

Parallel title — The title proper cited in another language and/or script.

Picture — A two-dimensional representation generally produced on an opaque backing. Includes the following formats:

Art print — An engraving, woodcut, etc. printed from the artist's plate.

Art reproduction — A copy of a work of art which has been mechanically reproduced.

Photograph — An image produced on a photo-sensitized surface by a camera.

Post card — A card for bearing a message through the mail without an envelope.

Poster — A bill or placard intended to be posted.

Study print — A picture with accompanying text which makes the print significant for study purposes.

Producer (Motion pictures) — The person with final responsibility for the making of a motion picture, including business aspects, management of the production, and the commercial success of the film.

Production company (Motion pictures) — The organization responsible for manufacture or production of a motion picture.

Program file — A machine-readable data file that contains the instructions that control the operation of a computer to produce the data as required.

Programmed instruction — An educational technique designed for self-instruction and testing, utilizing the sequencing of information into basic logical units, and providing the learner with knowledge of results.

Realia — Actual objects; artifacts, samples, specimens.

Relief map *see* **Map**

Relief globe *see* **Globe**

Relief model *see* **Map**

Sine loco (s.l.) — Without place; used to indicate the absence of the name of the place of publication.

Sine nomine (s.n.) — Without name; used to indicate the absence of the name of the publisher.

Slide — A small unit of transparent material containing an image, mounted in rigid format and designed for use in a slide viewer or projector. Presentation of special slides in pairs (stereographs) produces a three-dimensional effect.

Sound page — A two-dimensional opaque representation of printed or graphic material with integral sound.

Sound recording — A recording on which sound vibrations are registered by mechanical or electrical means so that the sound may be reproduced.

Specific material designation — A term indicating the class of material to which an item belongs, e.g., study print.

Specimen *see* **Realia**

Standard number — An internationally agreed upon standard number that uniquely identifies an item.

Standard title *see* Uniform title

Stereograph *see* **Slide**

Study print *see* **Picture**

Technical drawing — A plan, elevation, cross-section, detail, diagram, perspective, etc., made for use in an engineering, architectural or other technical context.

Transparency — An image produced on transparent material, designed for use with an overhead projector.

Uniform title — The particular title by which a work that has appeared under varying titles is to be identified for cataloguing purposes.

Videocassette *see* **Videorecording**

Videodisc *see* **Videorecording**

Videorecording — A recording designed for television playback, on which both pictures and sound have been registered electronically.

Videotape *see* **Videorecording**

Abbreviations

and others	et al.
black and white	b&w
centimetre(s)	cm.
circa	ca.
coloured	col.
copyright	c
Corporation	Corp.
Department	Dept.
diameter	diam.
edition(s)	ed., eds.
et alii	et al.
foot, feet	ft.
frame(s)	fr.
illustration(s)	ill.
inch(es)	in.
inches per second	ips
Incorporated	Inc. (use only in names of corporate bodies)
kilometre(s)	km.
Limited	Ltd. (use only in names of corporate bodies)
millimetre(s)	mm.
minute(s)	min.
monophonic	mono.
no name (of publisher)	s.n.
no place (of publication)	s.l.
number(s)	no.
opus	op.
page(s)	p.
part	pt.
photographs(s)	photo., photos.
projection	proj. (use only for cartographic materials)
quadraphonic	quad.
revised	rev.
revolutions per minute	rpm
second(s)	sec.
silent	si.
sine loco	S.l.
sine nomine	s.n.
sound	sd.
stereophonic	stereo.

Storage 5

General Suggestions for the Storage of an Integrated Collection

It is impossible to predict future developments in the rapidly changing media field. Storage requirements vary for different media centres and no single storage system is applicable to all. Manufacturers will continue to develop new equipment in response to media centres' needs.

The following guidelines apply to an integrated media centre, i.e., one which uses a single subject analysis system for all media and maintains an all-media catalogue.

1. All circulating materials are stored together in one room or complex of rooms. Nonbook materials should not be relegated to a separate room, particularly one accessible only to the media centre staff.
2. Open display storage is used for all materials, wherever possible. Storage in drawers and cabinets should be reduced to a minimum.
3. Rigid partitioning should be avoided. Flexible storage provides ease in interfiling classified items.
4. When media must be stored in containers, transparent materials are recommended for packaging. For instance, realia can be stored in clear plastic boxes.

Enclosed and inconvenient storage involves an uneconomical use of staff time and an unnecessary delay in service.

Total Intershelving

Intershelving of all materials is the ideal arrangement for collections which may be browsed by the public. It results in more frequent, more effective use of all materials by bringing to the patrons' attention the interrelationship of media. However, if the theft of a particular medium, e.g., sound tape cassettes, is a problem, dummy containers can be intershelved and the items stored in a supervised area.

Many materials are received in packages which can be shelved easily. A variety of containers is available commercially for media which are acquired either without or with unsuitable cartons.

Materials which arrive in unwieldy cartons may be repackaged. Some media centres have acquired suitable inexpensive containers cut to their specifications from local carton manufacturers. If media centres buy such packaging collectively, the price per container may be reduced to only a few cents. These cartons are assembled easily by the media centre staff as needed. The still-to-be-assembled containers do not take much storage space since they can be stored flat.

Uninteresting looking packaging may discourage circulation. There are several ways to make containers more attractive:

1. Keep the colourful publisher's brochure or catalogue after the item has been ordered and paste it to the container when the item is being processed.
2. Paste an extra catalogue card, particularly one with a summary, to the outside of the container.
3. Encourage art students in a school media centre to design appropriate and attractive packaging.

Partial Intershelving

Because of packaging, intershelving may consume more space than specialized shelving for each medium. For media centres which do not have sufficient storage space to allow total intershelving, the following suggestions for partial intershelving are offered:

1. Individual multimedia shelves which can be placed throughout the regular book shelves are available commercially. These shelves enable the media centre to locate all the nonbook materials on a given subject together on one or two shelves contiguous to books on the same subject.
2. Book ends which serve as containers for the smaller media, such as filmstrips and sound tape cassettes, are available commercially. Such materials can then be stored very near their proper place in the classification scheme.

3. Bins for sound discs, pamphlet boxes and/or Princeton files containing materials in a subject field can be placed on shelves at the end of the classification numbers relating to that field.
4. Book trucks can be fitted to house nonbook materials, so that nonbook materials in a given subject area may be placed near the book shelves containing the same subject.

Segregated Shelving
Archival collections must be kept in conditions best suited to the preservation of a particular medium. Intershelving may then be a lesser consideration. Any media centre which does not provide direct public access to its collection may not need to intershelve its material.

If a media centre's collection is not intershelved, or if part of its collection is held in other buildings, the entries for all its materials should still be interfiled in one catalogue in an area readily accessible to the public. In addition to this all-media catalogue, individual collections in other buildings or areas may have their own catalogues.

Bibliography of Practical Comments on Intershelving
The following items have been listed here rather than in the composite bibliography because of the great interest which has been expressed in intershelving. Only items with very practical content have been selected; those with a more theoretical slant will be found in the bibliography which starts on page 128. These items have been chosen for their intershelving content only, not for their comments on cataloguing.

Funk, Grace E. "Where do I look for it? On the mechanics of the integrated collection." *Bookmark*, 16, no. 5 (January 1975) pp. 13–17.

Hart, Thomas L. "Dare to integrate." *Audiovisual Instruction*, 21, no. 8 (October 1976) pp. 18–19.

Hart, Thomas L., comp. and ed. "Integrated shelving of multimedia collections." *School Media Quarterly*, 5, no. 1 (Fall 1976) pp. 19–30.

Langrehr, John S. and Anne Russell. "Audiovisual packaging and shelving." *Audiovisual Instruction*, 22, no. 9 (November 1977) pp. 12–14.

One-stop shopping (Kit) : *organizing media for accessibility*. Stout Menomonie, Wis.: Produced by Instructional Technology Services, University of Wisconsin for Wisconsin Association of School Libraries, c1975. 1 book, 1 filmstrip, 1 sound tape cassette and manual.

Stoness, B. Jeanne. "Integration of print and non-print resources." *Expression*, 1, no. 1 (Spring 1976) pp. 34–37.

Tiffany, Constance J. "The war between the stacks." *American Libraries*, 9, no. 8 (September 1978) p. 499.

Veihman, Robert A. "Some thoughts on intershelving." *Audiovisual Instruction*, 18, no. 3 (March 1973) pp. 87–88.

GENERAL GUIDELINES FOR THE CARE, HANDLING, AND STORAGE OF FILM MEDIA (Filmstrips, Microforms, Motion Pictures, Slides, Transparencies)

Care
Film should be cleaned and inspected after each use. Infrequently used film should be inspected regularly.

Film transport and optical equipment must be kept clean and dust-free.

Only qualified staff should attempt to repair either equipment or film.

Handling
Film must be kept away from sources of dust and objects which can scratch or tear it.

Film should not be jarred or dropped. Such treatment may produce cinch marks (short scratches) throughout the length of the film. Bent containers or reels can damage film severely.

Film should be handled only by the edges and should not be twisted.

Film must never get wet.

Film should be allowed to reach room temperature before it is screened.

Projection and viewing equipment must be mounted safely and all power cords secured.

The operator must not leave the machine while motion pictures are being projected or rewound. At the first sign of trouble, the projector must be stopped and rethreaded if necessary. If film *must* be re-fastened, *only* tape which will not remove the emulsion should be used.

Storage

Temperature: Film must not be stored in direct sunlight or near sources of heat. It should not be subjected to temperature changes of more than 20 degrees F. (11 degrees C.). 70 degrees F. (21 degrees C.) is optimum storage temperature, but extremes of 60 degrees F. (16 degrees C.) and 90 degrees F. (32 degrees C.) are tolerable.

Humidity: 50% relative humidity provides the ideal storage environment for film. The normal humidity range in a media centre is tolerable. Polyesterfilm will not dry out as quickly as other types.

Container: Film should be stored in dust-proof containers. These should be carefully selected to ensure that they are not composed of materials harmful to film, such as acid, sulphur, or peroxide.

Film stored on reels should be secured with a tape which will not remove the emulsion, e.g., masking tape. Rubber bands must not be used unless they have been specially manufactured without sulphur, and are loose enough to allow for expansion and contraction without cinching the film.

GENERAL GUIDELINES FOR THE CARE, HANDLING, AND STORAGE OF MAGNETIC TAPE (Sound tapes, sound tracks of various media, videotapes)

Care
In archival collections a tape which has not been used for a year should be rewound.

Handling
The tape itself should be touched as little as possible.

Storage

Temperature and Humidity: Extremes should be avoided in the storage area. Temperature may range from 40 degrees F. (4 degrees C.) to 80 degrees F. (27 degrees C.), relative humidity from 30% to 60%. Ideal conditions for archival storage are 70 degrees F. (21 degrees C.) and 50% relative humidity.

Container and shelving: Magnetic tapes should be stored in dust-proof containers, standing on edge, with proper supports to prevent their falling.

The storage area and/or shelving must not be subject to vibrations and must be free of all magnetic fields.

GENERAL GUIDELINES FOR THE CARE, HANDLING, AND STORAGE OF MICROSCOPE SLIDES

Microscope slides can withstand normal media centre usage and storage conditions, if during their construction the mounting medium has been allowed to dry properly. Slides should not be stored in direct sunlight, which might crack or melt resins and fade stains.

Ideal conditions for collections of valuable slides would include, in addition to the above, storage in areas of cool temperatures (60 to 65 degrees F. or 16° to 18°C.) and low humidity.

GENERAL GUIDELINES FOR THE CARE, HANDLING, AND STORAGE OF SOUND DISCS

Care
Discs must be kept free of dust and dirt. Distilled water applied with a lint-free cloth is the most economical and efficient method of cleaning discs. Mechanical cleaning devices may be purchased.

Stereophonic and quadraphonic grooves are easily damaged by heavy tone arms, improper anti-skate adjustment, or styli which are worn or the wrong size. Media centre playback equipment must be maintained by qualified personnel.

Handling
Discs should be handled as little as possible and then only by the edges.

Storage

Temperature: Discs should be kept at a stable temperature of about 70 degrees F. (21 degrees C.). Excessive heat (especially direct sunlight) will cause them to warp within a matter of hours.

Humidity: Discs will attract dust when humidity is low enough to cause a build-up of static electricity.

Shelving: Discs should never be stored so that they are supporting the weight of other discs. They should be shelved standing on edge, spine out, if they are not used frequently. For short term storage in a rapidly circulating collection, browser bins allow maximum access with minimum damage.

Intershelving of sound discs with other materials is facilitated by individual bins attached to book shelving. These bins, which are available commercially, may be pulled out for browsing convenience.

117

GENERAL GUIDELINES FOR THE STORAGE OF THREE-DIMENSIONAL MATERIALS (Dioramas, games, globes, kits, models, realia)

Because of diversity in shape and composition, no general guidelines have been included for the care and handling of three-dimensional materials.

Wherever possible, three-dimensional materials should be shelved with or near other media in the same subject field. The storage container should be as descriptive as possible of its contents. If the producer's container is colourful, descriptive, durable, and not over large in comparison to its contents, intershelve in this container. If, however, the producer's container does not conform to at least two of these requirements or if the item has been acquired without a suitable container, materials should be stored in transparent containers which will allow the media centre user to browse the collection. Alternatively, any type of container may be used if it is labelled with a description, and possibly a picture, of the contents. Adequate labelling will allow browsing of opaque containers.

GENERAL GUIDELINES FOR THE CARE, HANDLING, AND STORAGE OF TWO-DIMENSIONAL, OPAQUE MATERIALS (Charts, flash cards, maps, pictures)

Time and money should not be spent on the care of uncatalogued, ephemeral materials. The following guidelines apply to catalogued media which are part of a permanent collection.

Many books and pamphlets have been written about the care and storage of art prints, pictures, photographs, etc. Media centres with valuable materials should consult authoritative texts for advice about their preservation. These books should also be read for a fuller discussion of points listed below.

These brief guidelines apply to items in a permanent collection which are not very valuable or rare and which circulate with other media centre materials.

1. Some recommended methods to make fragile materials more durable are indicated below:

    Edging. The life of a map, picture, or similar material will be lengthened if it is edged with acetate fibre. Manual edging machines are available commercially.

    Lamination. Laminating equipment is now used by media centres for many purposes, e.g., covering book jackets.

    Mounting. The mounting materials must be acid-free.

    Spraying. Clear acrylic may be sprayed on the surface of pictures to protect them from finger marks, dirt, etc.

    Vinyl picture covers. These are useful for circulating fragile two-dimensional materials.

2. Dirt and grease from fingers and other sources can damage two-dimensional, opaque materials. Therefore, they should be stored in envelopes made of acid-free materials.

3. It is unwise to use most pressure sensitive tapes because they will discolour paper with a stain which is impossible to remove.

4. Newspaper clippings can be kept in their original form if they are backed with 100% rag mounting and stored in folders made of acid-free paper.

5. Photographs are particularly vulnerable to careless handling.

    a) Rubber cement or other rubber compounds, gummed or plastic tape can damage photographs. Dry mounting tissue should be used.

    b) Excessive heat and humidity should be avoided. (Negatives should be stored in metal, polyethylene, or styrene because wood and cardboard absorb moisture)

    c) Dirt, dust, light, and finger marks can cause deterioration. Photographs should be stored individually in seamless cellulose acetate envelopes or seamless all-rag envelopes.

    d) Writing on the back of photographs produces undesirable ridges on the face of the picture. Descriptive material should be typed on a separate sheet and placed in the envelope with the photograph.

Storage of Two-Dimensional Materials (including Transparencies)

Many two-dimensional materials are produced in containers suitable for intershelving. These include sets of transparencies in boxes or binders and similar materials. Single items of slight depth easily overlooked by the media centre patron should be shelved in brightly coloured acid-free envelopes.

Some two-dimensional materials need additional treatment before they can be intershelved. Maps with covers shelve easily; only the folds need reinforcing to prolong life. Where surface creases are tolerable, flat materials such as charts and maps should be folded rather than rolled, and the folds reinforced with suitable material. These folded items may then be placed in a manilla envelope, transparent bag, or box and intershelved with the rest of the collection.

A large collection of maps or other flat materials, which is not intershelved with other media, and unmounted materials which must be preserved uncreased should be filed flat where possible, and stored in waist-high horizontal map cases. This type of storage enables items to be consulted on top of the cases and minimizes handling.

Large-sized, mounted materials should be housed on open display devices. Such storage is being produced by many manufacturers in response to the fad for posters.

Appendices 6

Appendix A — Notes

It is impossible to provide cataloguing rules for all the materials which may be in a collection as well as for new formats which do not exist at this writing. When the *Anglo-American Cataloguing Rules*, 2nd edition, does not provide rules for a particular format, the cataloguer must use an appropriate rule(s) for other media as a guideline. The following notes are added to show the cataloguer the types of problems encountered in applying the *Anglo-American Cataloguing Rules*, 2nd edition, and the authors' methods of dealing with them.

The term "authors' suggestion" indicates that the authors have searched the *Anglo-American Cataloguing Rules*, 2nd edition, (cited as AACR/2), *ISBD(NBM): International Standard Bibliographic Descriptions for Non-Book Materials* (cited as ISBD(NBM)), *Nonbook Materials: the Organization of Integrated Collections*, 1st edition, (cited as NBM/1), the *Anglo-American Cataloging Rules*, Chapters 12 revised and 14 revised (cited as AACR 12 & AACR 14), *Non-Book Materials Cataloguing Rules* (cited as NBMCR), *Standards for Cataloging Nonprint Materials*, 4th edition, (cited as SCNM/4), and *ISBD(CM): International Standard Bibliographic Description for Cartographic Materials* (cited as ISBD(CM)) for guidance and found none. The proposed solutions are the result of discussions with media specialists and common sense.

The word "author(s)" has been used frequently throughout this book for the sake of economy of words. It is used in the sense defined on page   .

Because some items had parts missing or the producers sent brochures rather than the actual items, the authors supplied what they considered to be appropriate information on sample cards 11, 12, 62, 93, 110, and 126. Sample cards 40, 41, and 42 were supplied by the University of British Columbia Library.

1. "Media code" in this book means symbols used in conjunction with a call number to indicate type of material, e.g., FS 599.2. Please note that the term "media code" has another meaning when used in automated cataloguing.
2. The general material designation has been added as a minimum requirement because of the policy decision in this book to use a general material designation for all catalogue records.
3. Drawn from NBM/1.
4. Authors' interpretation of "first part" 1.0H (multipart items) applied to nonbook materials.
5. "container which is the unifying element" — 8.0B1.
6. Authors' suggestion. This problem has been raised frequently.
7. Authors' suggestion based on 1.1F2 and AACR 12, rule 225C3 & NBMCR, rule 4.
8. 3.1G1 & 3.1G4, 6.1G1 & 6.1G4, 7.1G1 & 7.1G4, 11.1G1 & 11.1G4 allow this method; 8.1G1 & 10.1G1 do not. This seems inconsistent and therefore has been made a general rule in this book.
9. 1.0A2, 3.1G1 & 3.1G5, and 8.1B2 have been extended to all materials.
10. The only chapter in AACR/2 which does not allow the omission of the specific material designation or a prefix when a general material designation is used is Chapter 8, Graphics. This seems inconsistent and so this provision has been extended to all media. In actual fact, the only media from Chapter 8 to which this will apply are flash cards and filmstrips.

    The national libraries of Australia, Canada, Great Britain, and the United States have agreed not to adopt this option because these four agencies will have different practices regarding the use of general material designations. Therefore, they decided to apply the most complete rules for extent of item. In this book, the authors decided to apply the option for almost all 1st level and some 2nd level description.
11. Phrase "or smaller" drawn from 3.5D1.
12. Authors' suggestion.
13. Measuring the container drawn from 3.5D5 & 10.5D2. This may be extended to all media if this is useful information.
14. Permission to repeat accompanying materials taken from 9.5D3, ISBD(NBM) and ISBD(CM).
15. Two-dimensional works of art are discussed in AACR/2, chapter 8 and three-dimensional works of art in chapter 10. Therefore, the rules here are drawn from both chapters.

16. 8.0B1 excludes the frame from being a chief source of information; 10.0B1 allows the item, accompanying material, and container to be chief sources. Because the title for most paintings, etc., is found on the mount or frame, the authors advocate the application of 10.0B1 to all art originals, and, therefore, have not indicated the chief source of information.

17. "number of overlays if transparent" taken from 8.5B4. This gives a more accurate description.

18. 8.5C6 has been applied generally to all charts. See sample card 9 where this information is necessary.

19. 8.5D6 has been applied generally to all charts. See sample card 9 where this information is necessary.

20. Place has been listed because producer/manufacturer and date are unknown. The summary was added to identify more precisely the content of the item.

21. "in descriptive case" rather than "in case" because the former implies an amount of information on the case.

    Numbering in contents note indicates arrangement of charts. #6 is on the verso of #1.

22. Preference given to title frames drawn from NBM/1.

23. Last numbered frame taken from 2.5B2, AACR 12, rule 228D1, & ISBD (NBM) 5.1.11.

24. "in square brackets" from 2.5B7.

25. Counting frames taken from AACR 12, rule 228D1.

26. "Stored in a ..." — The Bell & Howell cartridge can be opened as easily as an ordinary container and the filmstrip used with standard equipment. It seems misleading to list "1 filmstrip cartridge" in extent of item as this infers that the filmstrip must be used with special equipment.

27. "compiled and annotated" suggests authorship and the item is advertised in the publisher's catalogue as being Newton's work.

    Secondary position city in the country of the cataloguing agency named: If this were catalogued in the U.S., it would read London ; New York; if catalogued in the U.K., it would read London.

28. Sound if integral taken from 8.5C4, 8.5C12.

29. Compare this with sample card 35. The producers of both these items have named them flash cards on the packaging. Both items can be used two ways. In sample card 35 the item is catalogued as a kit because the media centre will use it either way. Here the item is catalogued as a flash card because the media centre staff judges that it will be used primarily as a flash card set.

30. "137 games on 154 cards" taken from 2.5B19, 3.5B2, 4.5B1 (optional addition).

31. Container, cradle, and stand have not been given a hierarchy in 3.0B2. This seems a sensible order.

32. 3.5B1 directs the cataloguer to use "globe" for globes other than celestial globes, but allows the use of "relief model." ISBD(CM) 5.1.2., NBM/1, SCNM/4, and partially NBMCR use the term "relief globe." The authors have retained this useful phrase.

33. The container looks to be an all-purpose package, that is, one in which all Nystrom relief globes are distributed. This seems an unsuitable title. The title is drawn by inference from the cassette title.

34. This section is drawn from 10.0H, 1.10, 1.0H.

    In NBM/1 a kit was defined as "two or more media, which are not fully interdependent and, therefore may be used separately." This meant that if a fully interdependent set was to be catalogued, a choice had to be made between the two interdependent media as to which one was dominant, and the set catalogued under the dominant medium with the subordinate medium listed at the end of the collation. The new definition here and in AACR/2 will necessitate a change in the cataloguing of such interdependent sets. Now a dominant medium will be chosen only if the "relative predominance of components is ... easily determinable." If in a particular instance the cataloguer is unsure of the predominant constituent, the item should be catalogued as a kit.

    Sample cards 37 and 91 are examples of the impact of the change in definition. Sample card 37 was catalogued in NBM/1 (sample card 109) as a slide because a choice had to be made between the components of the interdependent set. However, in this book it is considered a kit as neither slides nor sound disc are clearly predominant.

    Sample card 91 is an example of a unit in which one item is clearly predominant; the chart is of much less significance than the slides and teacher's guide. However, had this unit been included in NBM/1, it would have been catalogued as a kit because its components are largely independent.

35. 1.10C2a implies this order in the example.

36. "alphabetical order" drawn from ISBD(NBM), AACR 12, & NBM/1.

37. The bilingual title was not listed in NBM/1 because very little of the contents are bilingual. AACR/2 prescribes the listing of a bilingual title if one is given.

38. The only place listed on the item is "Canada." In this instance, one could guess correctly that Montreal is the place of production. However, "Canada" is given here as an example of 1.4C6 which shows only bracketed examples. This is not bracketed here because the word is taken from the chief source of information.

39. R. Way's name is only on the filmstrip manual, but the producer's catalogue states her to be the author of the kit as a whole.
AACR/2 gives no direction for placement of the series area when each medium is listed on a separate line. This is the authors' suggestion.

40. Drawn from NBM/1 & SCNM/4.

41. "ca. 1:7,200,000" is used here because the map states that the scale is approximate, and not because the scale was derived.
"(1 attached overlay)" drawn from 8.5B4, NBM/1, and SCNM/4.
Dimensions drawn from 3.5D1 and common sense.

42. It is possible to reproduce cartographic material, and serials (though less likely), in other media, e.g., a map on a transparency. If descriptive cataloguing is to be truly consistent, this area should be applied to maps and serials in any format. However, AACR/2 does not allow this.

43. 11.5B1 allows this only for microfiches. However, it seems consistent to apply this rule to microopaques as well. If it is useful information for the patron, add the number of frames to the extent of item in sample card 61.

44. "10 microopaques on 5 cards" drawn from 3.5B2.

45. "Hung from metal stand" taken from 3.5C5 & 3.5D4.
Order of notes — Despite the example in 10.1B6, these notes are accompanying material and should come under 10.7B11 and, therefore after 10.1B10 which deals with scale.

46. 7.5B1 applies this only to videorecordings. A trade name is also necessary for motion picture loop cartridges.

47. "(Technicolor)" is a projection requirement for a Technicolor projector, not a statement of colour process.

48. Drawn from 8.5B4.

49. These subject headings are not normally given to single works. However, they are useful in media centres where patrons ask for an example of particular types of art.

50. A summary rather than a contents note is given because 11 titles would make a long contents record and the same information can be conveyed succinctly in a few words.

51. "b&w and col." drawn from ISBD(NBM). Examples in AACR/2 suggest the predominance of one or the other.

52. Because flannel board pieces can be moved, size is not given. Authors' suggestion.

53. "method of preservation" and sample card 88 "dried" likened to process in 8.5C2 and method of reproduction in 8.5C3 & 8.5C15.

54. Authors' interpretation of 8.0B1.

55. AACR/2 gives directions for sound slides only (8.5C12). This has been extended to stereographs because there seems to be no reason why a producer could not market sound stereographs.

56. Separating credits between statement of responsibility and notes drawn from 7.1F1 & 7.7B6.

57. "glass" drawn from 10.5C1.

58. "1 sound recording (36 min.)" drawn from 7.5B1.

59. There are no rules in AACR/2 for sound pages. The authors have adapted the rules for sound recordings, but are not entirely satisfied with the result. If the rules had been followed more strictly, the extent of item would have read "54 sound p. (ca. 216 min.)." The term "sound pages" was used to make this more intelligible, since "pages" are not normally associated with sound recordings. The authors would be interested in receiving comments and suggestions about how to catalogue sound pages using AACR/2.

60. The rules for technical drawings in AACR/2, Chapter 8 do not seem complete enough to satisfy the needs of engineering libraries. Therefore, the authors have expanded this section. Of our source documents, only NBMCR dealt with technical drawings, and we found it to be only partially helpful. Most of the ideas for this section have come from the staff of media centres which contain technical drawings and from professional engineers who use them. The authors have attempted to fit these ideas into an AACR/2 framework.

If descriptive cataloguing is to be truly consistent, scale for technical drawings should be treated in the same manner as maps and listed in the mathematical data area. However, Chapter 8 does not provide rules for this area.

61. Authors' interpretation of 8.0B1 and common sense.

62. Sample cards 123A and 123B — "on 1 reel" drawn from 6.5B3, 7.5B3, 11.5B2. These rules do not deal directly with the problem of two separate works on a single physical unit. Dr. Ronald Hagler, Chairperson of the Canadian Committee on Cataloguing, suggested this phrase as the one implied by the examples.

63. Sample card 124 — "1 videorecording" (7.5B1) is given in the extent of item because two formats (1 reel and 1 cassette) are listed on the card. Dimensions are not given in extent of item because of the difference in the two formats.

Two call numbers are given here as an example for those media centres which assign unique numbers. Media centres which do not have such a policy would assign one number only (see sample cards 79, 109). The authors have chosen the work mark "u" for the "U-Matic" format and the work mark "h" for the ½-in. format.

64. This section has been drawn from 6.11, 8.4A2, 10.4C2, 10.4D2 and 10.4F2.

65. Sample card 128 — "Women in motion pictures." In 1981 the Library of Congress plans to change the subject heading "Women in moving-pictures" to this.

Appendix B

GENERAL MATERIAL DESIGNATIONS LISTED IN THE *Anglo-American Cataloguing Rules*, 2nd. Ed.

A media centre may elect to use one of these lists of terms or to omit a general material designation from the catalogue record. See pages 9-10 and page 18 for a discussion about the use of general material designations.

North American terms	British terms		
globe	cartographic material	microform	microform
map		motion picture	motion picture
art original	graphic	kit	multimedia
chart		music*	printed music
filmstrip		diorama	object
flash card		game	
picture		microscope slide	
slide		model	
technical drawing		realia	
transparency		sound recording	sound recording
machine-readable data file	machine-readable data file	text*	text
manuscript*	manuscript	videorecording	videorecording

A third list of general material designations may be found in the various International Standard Bibliographic Descriptions published by the International Federation of Library Associations.

*"manuscript," "music," and "text" are not discussed in this book. Media centres which have elected to use general material designations should apply these terms to appropriate items.

Appendix C

At their January 1978 meeting, the American Library Association Resources and Technical Services Division Board of Directors adopted the following guidelines, which were developed by the Ad Hoc Subcommittee for the Subject Analysis of Audiovisual Materials.

GUIDELINES FOR THE SUBJECT ANALYSIS OF AUDIOVISUAL MATERIALS

1. Principles of Subject Heading Application

a) *Topical headings*. Topical headings should be applied to audiovisual materials whenever the subject content is explicit or implicit. Topical headings include those for people, places, things, historical events, abstract concepts, etc.

b) *Non-topical headings*. Non-topical subject headings, such as genre, e.g., "experimental films," and technique, e.g. "animation," should be assigned to audiovisual materials.

Both types of subject headings may be applied to the same audiovisual item, for example, an experimental motion picture about friendship may have the subject heading "Friendship" and the subject heading "Experimental film."

c) Multi-item sets and multi-subject items should be analyzed to whatever degree the individual item warrants. For example, a set of eight sound filmstrips on Africa with different countries discussed in each filmstrip, should have a heading for each country, as well as for Africa.

d) *Option*. General material designations may serve as form subdivisions. The precedent for this type of subdivision is seen in the existing form subdivisions "Dictionaries," "Indexes," "Periodicals." The need for this option is dependent on the collection size and the physical arrangement of the particular collection. The recommended authority for the subdivisions is the list of general material designations in the *Anglo-American Cataloguing Rules*, 2nd edition.

2. Subject Heading Authority Lists

a) Subject heading authority lists, e.g., *Sears List of Subject Headings* and *Library of Congress Subject Headings*, should provide guidance for the creation of subject headings where an appropriate one does not exist or has yet to be established. Audiovisual materials are often very current and require currency in subject analysis.

b) An explanation of the particulars and the peculiarities of audiovisual subject analysis should be provided in the subject heading authority lists, including a discussion of the matters here outlined.

c) All book-oriented form subdivisions and form-oriented headings should be changed to make them applicable to book and audiovisual materials. For example, "Guides" would be substituted for "Guide-books" and "Counting" substituted for "Counting books."

3. Classification Numbers and Their Authority

Classification numbers, e.g., Dewey Decimal or Library of Congress, should be extended to all audiovisual materials. Although the individual library may not physically integrate its collection, the assignment of classification numbers to audiovisual materials by individual libraries, central cataloging agencies, the Library of Congress, and others provides for the unification of materials in bibliographies, facilitates automated retrieval, allows for greater flexibility in physical arrangement, and encourages consistency in cataloging.

Bibliography

The following bibliography is an extension of the bibliography in the 1st edition. The only items which have been repeated from the 1st edition are standard works and new editions.

Akers, Susan Grey. *Aker's simple library cataloging*. 6th ed. completely revised and rewritten by Arthur Curley and Jana Varlejs. Metuchen, N.J.: Scarecrow Press, 1977.

American National Standards Committee on Library Work, Documentation, and Related Publishing Practices, Z39. Subcommittee 4 on Bibliographic References. *American national standard for bibliographic references*. New York: American National Standards Institute, 1977. (ANSI Z39.29-1977)

Anglo-American cataloguing rules... edited by Michael Gorman and Paul W. Winkler. Chicago: American Library Association, 1978.

Art library manual; a guide to resources and practice, edited by Philip Pacey. London: R.R. Bowker, in association with the Art Libraries Society, 1977.

Audiovisual media and libraries; selected readings, compiled by Emanuel T. Prostano. Littleton, Colo.: Libraries Unlimited, 1972.

Austin, Derek. *PRECIS; a manual of concept analysis and subject indexing*. London: Council of the British National Bibliography, 1974.

Austin, Judith. "The care and feeding of photograph collections." *Idaho Librarian*, 27 (January 1975) pp. 3–7.

Avedon, Don M. *The user's guide to standard microfiche formats*. 3d ed. Silver Spring, Md.: National Micrographics Association, 1976.

Bahr, Alice Harrison. *Microforms: the librarians' view, 1978-79*. White Plains, N. Y.: Knowledge Industry Publications, c1978. (The Professional librarian series)

Barnes, Shirley Louise. "Review of contemporary methods of cataloging non-print materials." Master's thesis, University of Oklahoma, 1974.

Bolt, Janice. "A brief look at the organization of instructional media." *Illinois Libraries*, 55, no. 7 (September 1973) pp. 494–497.

The Bookman's glossary. 5th ed. edited by Jean Peters. New York: R. R. Bowker, 1975.

British Standards Institution. *Glossary of documentation terms*. London: BSI, 1976. (BS5408:1976)

Brown, James W., Kenneth D. Norberg and Sara K. Srygley. *Administering educational media: instructional technology and library services*. 2d ed. New York: McGraw-Hill, 1972.

Buchanan, Brian. *A glossary of indexing terms*. London: C. Bingley, 1976.

Buth, Olga. "Scores and recordings." *Library Trends*, 23, no. 3 (January 1975) pp. 427–450.

Care and handling of magnetic tape. Redwood City, Calif.: Ampex, 1976.

Chibnall, Bernard. *The organisation of media*. London: C. Bingley, 1976.

Conners, Richard J. *Microfilm: active and vital*. St. Paul, Minn.: Minnesota Mining & Manufacturing, 1975.

Croghan, Antony. *A bibliographic system for non-book media; a description and list of works*. London: Coburgh Publications, 1976.

Croghan, Antony. *A code of rules for, with an exposition of, integrated cataloguing of non-book media*. London: Coburgh Publications, 1972.

Croghan, Antony. *A thesaurus-classification for the physical forms of non-book media*. 2d ed. London: Coburgh Publications, 1976. Microfiche.

Cunha, George Daniel Martin and Dorothy Grant Cunha. *Conservation of library materials; a manual and bibliography on the care, repair and restoration of library materials*. 2d ed. 2 vols. Metuchen, N. J.: Scarecrow Press, 1971-2.

Daily, Jay E. *Cataloging phonorecordings; problems and possibilities*. New York: M. Dekker, 1975. (Practical library and information science, v. 1)

Daily, Jay E. *Organizing nonprint materials; a guide for librarians*. New York: M. Dekker, 1972. (Books in library and information science, v. 3)

D'Alleyrand, Marc R. "Holograms: putting the third D into the catalog." *Wilson Library Bulletin*, 51, no. 9 (May 1977) pp. 746–750.

Dowell, Arlene Taylor. *Cataloging with copy; a decision-maker's handbook*. Littleton, Col.: Libraries Unlimited, 1976.

Dykstra, Mary. *Access to film information: an indexing and retrieval system for the National Film Board of Canada*. Halifax: Dalhousie

University School of Library Service, 1977. (Dalhousie University Libraries and Dalhousie University School of Library Service. Occasional paper 15)

The Elementary school library collection; a guide to books and other media, phases 1-2-3. Edited by Phyllis Van Orden, assisted by Mary V. Gaver and others. 10th ed. New Brunswick, N. J.: Bro-Dart Foundation, 1976.

Expanding media, edited by Deirdre Boyle. Phoenix, Ariz.: Oryx Press, 1977.

Foster, Donald L. *Prints in the public library*. Metuchen, N.J.: Scarecrow Press, 1973.

Fothergill, Richard and Ian Butchart. *Non-book materials in libraries; a practical guide*. London: C. Bingley, 1978.

Freeman, Patricia. *Pathfinder; an operational guide for the school librarian*. New York: Harper & Row, c1975.

Gaddy, Dale. *A microform handbook*. Silver Spring, Md.: National Microfilm Association, 1974.

Gaeddert, Barbara Knisely. *The classification and cataloging of sound recordings: an annotated bibliography*. Ann Arbor: Music Library Association, 1977. (MLA Technical reports, no. 4)

Gibson, Bob. "An introduction to micropublishing." *Canadian library progress; a selection of the best writings from Canadian library publications*, 2 (1974) pp. 336—342.

Gray, Robert A. "Watch out for videodiscs in your future." *Audiovisual Instruction*, 23, no. 9 (December 1978) p. 19.

Gunter, Jonathan F. *Super 8: the modest medium*. Paris: Unesco, c1976 (Monographs on communication technology and utilization, 1)

Hagler, Ronald. *Where's that rule?; a cross-index of the two editions of the Anglo-American cataloguing rules*. Ottawa: Canadian Library Association, 1979.

Halsey, Richard Sweeney. *Classical music recordings for home and library*. Chicago: American Library Association, 1976.

Handling, repair, and storage of 16 mm motion picture films. Lincolnwood, Ill.: Research Technology Inc., 1977.

Handling special materials in libraries; a project of the South Atlantic Chapter, SLA, edited by Frances E. Kaiser. New York: Special Libraries Association, 1974.

Harmon, Robert B. *Simplified cataloging manual for small libraries and private collections*. San Jose, Calif.: Bibliographic Research Library, 1975. (Bibliographic Research Library, publication no. 2)

Harpp, David N. "An inexpensive filmstrip system." *Journal of Chemical Education*, 54, no. 5 (May 1977) pp. 307—308.

Harrison, Helen P. *Film library techniques*. London: Focal Press, 1973.

Harrod, Leonard Montague. *The librarians' glossary of terms used in librarianship, documentation, and the book crafts, and reference book*. 4th rev. ed. Boulder, Colo.: Westview Press, 1977.

Haycock, Ken and Lynne Isberg. *Sears list of subject headings: Canadian companion*. New York: H. W. Wilson, 1978.

Hicks, Warren B. and Alma M. Tillin. *Managing multimedia libraries*. New York: R. R. Bowker, 1977.

Hill, Donna. *The picture file; a manual and a curriculum-related subject heading list*. 2d ed. rev. and enl. Hamden, Conn.: Linnet Books, 1978.

Hill, Janet Swan. "Developments in map cataloging at the Library of Congress." *Special Libraries*, 68, no. 4 (April 1977) pp. 149—154.

Hoffmann, Helen. "The choice of main entry for sound recordings." *International Cataloguing*, 7, no. 1 (January/March 1978) pp. 5—7.

Holmes, John. *Preservation and restoration; a brief history, and an account of work being done at Mills Memorial Library, McMaster University*. Hamilton, Ont.: Cromlech Press, 1975. (Library research news, 2: no. 3, June 1973)

How to start an audiovisual collection, edited by Myra Nadler. Metuchen, N.J.: Scarecrow Press, 1978.

Hudson, Alice C. "Conversion to automated cataloging at the Map Division, NYPL." *Special Libraries*, 67, no. 2 (February 1976) pp. 97—101.

The Integration of nonprint media. Washington, D.C.: Association of Research Libraries, Systems and Procedures Exchange Center, 1977. (SPEC kit 33)

International Federation of Library Associations and Institutions. Joint Working Group on the International Standard Bibliographic Description for Cartographic Materials. *ISBD(CM); international standard bibliographic description for cartographic materials*. London: IFLA International Office for UBC, 1977.

International Federation of Library Associations and Institutions. Joint Working Group on the International Standard Bibliographic Description for Serials. *ISBD(S); international standard bibliographic description for serials*. 1st standard ed. London: IFLA International Office for UBC, 1977.

International Federation of Library Associations and Institutions. Working Group on the International Standard Bibliographic Description. *ISBD(NBM); international standard bibliographic description for non-book materials*. London: IFLA International Office for UBC, 1977.

International Symposium on the Cataloguing, Coding and Statistics of Audio-Visual Materials, Strasbourg, 1976. Proceedings, organized by ISO/TC 46 Documentation in collaboration with IFLA and IFTC, 7-9 January, 1976 in Strasbourg. Paris: Unesco, 1976.

Irvine, Betty Jo. "Organization and management of art slide collections." *Library Trends*, 23, no. 3 (January 1975) pp. 401–416.

Irvine, Betty Jo. *Slide libraries; a guide for academic institutions and museums*. Littleton, Colo.: Libraries Unlimited, 1974.

Korty, Margaret Barton. *Audio-visual materials in the church library; how to select, catalog, process, store, circulate, and promote*. Riverdale, Md.: Church Library Council, c1977.

Lamy-Rousseau, Françoise. *Traitement automatisé des documents multi-media avec les systèmes ISBD unifié, Lamy-Rousseau et precis, propositions S.I.L.P.* Quebec: Ministère de l'Education, 1974.

Larsgaard, Mary. *Map librarianship; an introduction*. Littleton, Colo.: Libraries Unlimited, 1978.

Lerner, Fred. "A classified vertical file." *The U*n*a*b*a*s*h*e*d librarian, 26 (1978) pp. 3–4.

Library Association. Media Cataloguing Rules Committee. *Non-book materials cataloguing rules; integrated code of practice and draft revision of the Anglo-American cataloguing rules, British text, part III*. London: National Council for Educational Technology with The Library Association, 1973.

Library of Congress. MARC Development Office. *Maps, a MARC format; specifications for magnetic tapes containing catalog records for maps*. 2d ed. Washington, D.C.: 1976.

Library of Congress. Subject Cataloging Division. *Library of Congress subject headings*. 2 vols. 8th ed. Washington, D.C.: 1975.

Limbacher, James B. *A reference guide to audiovisual information*. New York: R. R. Bowker, 1972.

Loertscher, David V. *A nonbook cataloging sampler*. Austin, Tex.: Armadillo Press, 1975. (Applications of library science, v. 5)

McLean, Isabel K. *Non-print resources; a study of Ontario public and regional library systems*. Ottawa: Canadian Library Association, 1975.

McNally, Paul. "The organization and service of an audiovisual collection in college libraries." *Australian Academic and Research Libraries*, no. 3 (March 1972) pp. 33–47.

Map librarianship: readings, compiled by Roman Drazniowsky. Metuchen, N.J.: Scarecrow Press, 1975.

Massonneau, Suzanne. "Developments in the organization of audiovisual materials." *Library Trends*, 25, no. 3 (January 1977) pp. 665–684.

Merrett, Christopher Edmond. *Map cataloguing and classification; a comparison of approaches*. [Sheffield, Eng.]: University of Sheffield, 1976. (University of Sheffield Postgraduate School of Librarianship and Information Science occasional publications series, number 7)

Microforms in libraries; a reader, edited by Albert James Diaz. Weston, Conn.: Microform Review Inc., 1975.

Midgley, Thomas Keith. "21 oddball ideas that work." *Audiovisual Instruction*, 21, no. 7 (September 1976) pp. 43, 63.

National Center for Education Statistics. *Educational technology; a handbook of standard terminology and a guide for recording and reporting information about educational technology*. Washington, D.C.: U.S. Dept. of Health, Education, and Welfare, Education Division, National Center for Education Statistics, 1975. (State educational records and reports series, handbook X)

National Microfilm Association. *Introduction to micrographics*. Silver Spring, Md.: N.M.A., 1973.

New, Peter G. *Reprography for librarians*. London: C. Bingley, 1975.

Nichols, Harold. *Map librarianship*. London: C. Bingley, 1976.

Noble, Valerie. "Business information audio cassettes: their care and feeding." *Special Libraries*, 64, no. 10 (October 1973) pp. 419–422.

Nonbook materials; a bibliography of recent publications, edited by Hans Wellisch. [College Park, Md.] : College of Library and Information Services, University of Maryland, 1975. (Student contribution series, no. 6)

Nonprint media in academic libraries, edited by Pearce S. Grove. Chicago: American Library Association, 1975. (ACRL Publications in librarianship, no. 34)

Non-print media problems; proceedings of a pre-conference workshop sponsored by the

Canadian Association of College and University Libraries held at Winnipeg, June 22-23, 1974, edited by Anne Woodsworth. Ottawa: Canadian Library Association, 1975. (CLA Occasional paper, no. 83)

Piercy, Esther J. *Commonsense cataloging; a manual for the organization of books and other materials in school and small public libraries*. 2d ed. rev. by Marian Sanner. New York: H.W. Wilson, 1974.

Planning and operating media centres; readings from Audiovisual Instruction, 2. Washington, D.C.: Association for Educational Communications and Technology, 1975.

Prostano, Emanuel T. *School media programs; case studies in management*. 2d ed. Metuchen, N.J.: Scarecrow Press, 1974.

Public Library Association. Audiovisual Committee. *Guidelines for audiovisual materials and services for large public libraries*. Chicago: American Library Association, 1975.

Public Library Association. Audiovisual Committee. *Recommendations for audiovisual materials and services for small and medium-sized public libraries*. Chicago: American Library Association, 1975.

Quinly, William J. *The selection, acquisition, and utilization of audiovisual materials*. 2d ed. Pullman, Wash.: Information Futures, 1978.

Ravilious, C.P. *A survey of existing systems and current proposals for the cataloguing and description of non-book materials collected by libraries, with preliminary suggestions for their international co-ordination*. Paris: Unesco, 1975. (Com. 75/WS/5)

Reader in media, technology and libraries, edited by Margaret Chisholm with Dennis D. McDonald. Englewood, Colo.: Microcard Editions Books, 1975. (Reader series in library and information science)

Reader in music librarianship, edited by Carol June Bradley. Washington, D.C.: Microcard Editions Books, 1973.

Redfern, Brian. *Organizing music in libraries*. Rev. ed. 2 vols. London: C. Bingley, 1978-9.

Rehrauer, George. *The film user's handbook; a basic manual for managing library film services*. New York: R.R. Bowker, 1975.

Reichmann, Felix and Josephine M. Tharpe. *Bibliographic control of microforms*. With the cooperation of Henriette Avram [and others]; sponsored by the Association of Research Libraries under contract with the Office of Education. Westport, Conn.: Greenwood Press, 1972.

Rice, James. "There's a videodisc in your future." *Library Journal*, 103, no. 2 (January 15, 1978) pp. 143—144.

Roberts, Don. "If you want non-print media, don't look in the catalog!" *Hennepin County Library Cataloging Bulletin*, no. 26 (February 1, 1977) pp. 10—13.

Rogers, JoAnn V. "Cataloging nonprint materials in school media centers." *School Library Journal*, 24, no. 8 (April 1978) pp. 51—53.

Rogers, JoAnn V. "Nonprint cataloging; a call for standardization." *American Libraries*, 10, no. 1 (January 1979) pp. 46—48.

Roldan, Gonzalo. *Suggestions for organizing and administering a media library*. Waukegan, Ill.: Luxor Corp., [197—]

Rosenberg, Kenyon C. and John S. Doskey. *Media equipment; a guide and dictionary*. Littleton, Colo.: Libraries Unlimited, 1976.

Rufsvold, Margaret I. *Guides to educational media; films, filmstrips, multimedia kits, programmed instruction materials, recordings on discs and tapes, slides, transparencies, videotapes*. 4th ed. Chicago: American Library Association, 1977.

Rules for the brief cataloging of music in the Library of Congress; exceptions to the Anglo-American cataloging rules. Ann Arbor, Mich.: Music Library Association, 1970.

Saffady, William. *Micrographics*. Littleton, Colo.: Libraries Unlimited, 1978.

Salm, Walter G. *Cassette tape recorders, how they work — care and repair*. Blue Ridge Summit, Pa.: Tab Books, 1973.

Schwarz, Philip John. "Keyword indexing of non-book media." *Audiovisual Instruction*, 19, no. 9 (November 1974) pp. 84—87.

Sears, Minnie Earl. *Sears list of subject headings*. 11th ed. edited by Barbara M. Westby. New York: H.W. Wilson, 1977.

Shifrin, Malcolm. *Information in the school library; an introduction to the organisation of non-book materials*. London: C. Bingley, 1973.

Spaulding, Carl M. "Kicking the silver habit: confessions of a former addict." *American Libraries*, 9, no. 11 (December 1978) pp. 653—699.

Spigai, Frances G. *The invisible medium: the state of the art of microform and a guide to the literature*. Washington, D.C.: American Society for Information Science, 1973.

Storage and handling of aperture cards, copy cards and camera cards. Pine City, Minn.: 3M, [1977?]

Storage & preservation of microfilms. Rochester, N.Y.: Eastman Kodak, [197—]. (Kodak pamphlet, no. D-31)

Taggart, Dorothy T. *A guide to sources in educational media*. Metuchen, N.J.: Scarecrow Press, 1975.

Tansey, Luraine. "Classification of research photographs and slides." *Library Trends*, 23, no. 3 (January 1975) pp. 417–426.

Teague, S. J. *Microform librarianship*. London: Butterworths, 1977.

Tillin, Alma M. *School library media center procedures*. Madison, Wis.: Demco Educational Corp., 1973.

Tillin, Alma M. and William J. Quinly. *Standards for cataloging nonprint materials; an interpretation and practical application*. 4th ed. Washington, D.C.: Association for Educational Communications and Technology, 1976.

Toys to go; a guide to the use of realia in public libraries, editors, Faith H. Hektoen, Jeanne R. Rinehart. Chicago: American Library Association, 1976.

Weihs, Jean Riddle. "Nonbook cataloging: problems and prospects." *Hennepin County Library Cataloging Bulletin*, no. 29 (July/August 1977) pp. 36-42.

Weihs, Jean Riddle. "Problems of subject analysis for audio/visual materials in Canadian libraries." *Canadian Library Journal*, 33, no. 5 (October 1976) pp. 453, 455.

Wilson, De Etta. "On the way to intershelving: elements in the decision." *Hawaii Library Association Journal*, 33 (1976) pp. 43–51.

Wynar, Bohdan S. *Introduction to cataloging and classification*. 5th ed. prepared with the assistance of John Phillip Immroth. Littleton, Colo.: Libraries Unlimited, 1976. (Library science text series)

Index

DATE DUE

GAYLORD			PRINTED IN U.S.A.